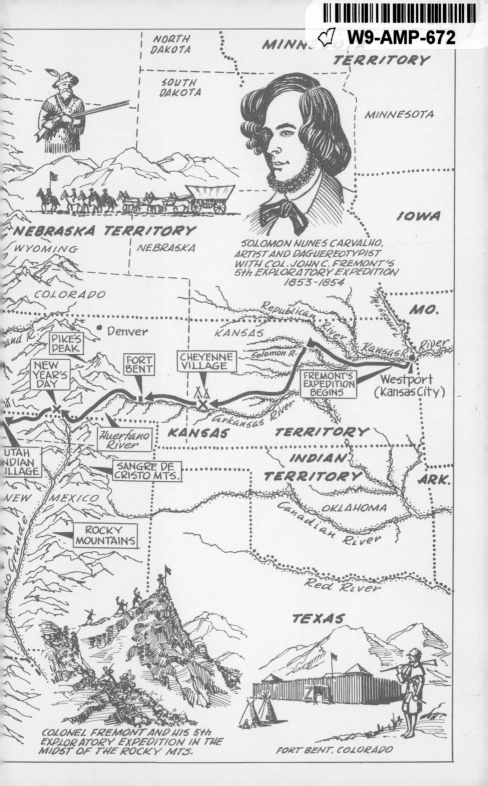

NORTH DAKOTA

SOUTH DAKOTA

MINNESOTA TERRITORY

MINNESOTA

IOWA

NEBRASKA TERRITORY

WYOMING

NEBRASKA

COLORADO

SOLOMON NUNES CARVALHO, ARTIST AND DAGUEREOTYPIST WITH COL. JOHN C. FREMONT'S 5th EXPLORATORY EXPEDITION 1853-1854

MO.

• Denver

Republican River

Missouri River

Kansas R. River

KANSAS

Solomon R.

PIKE'S PEAK

FORT BENT

CHEYENNE VILLAGE

FREMONT'S EXPEDITION BEGINS

Westport (Kansas City)

NEW YEAR'S DAY

Arkansas River

Huerfano River

KANSAS TERRITORY

UTAH INDIAN VILLAGE

SANGRE DE CRISTO MTS.

INDIAN TERRITORY

ARK.

NEW MEXICO

OKLAHOMA

Canadian River

ROCKY MOUNTAINS

Rio Grande

Red River

TEXAS

COLONEL FREMONT AND HIS 5th EXPLORATORY EXPEDITION IN THE MIDST OF THE ROCKY MTS.

FORT BENT, COLORADO

Sophie Greenspan

Fremont

Carvalho

OCIETY OF AMERICA

Westward with

The Story of Solomo

THE JEWISH PUBLICATIO

Philadelphia/ 5729 · 1969

Westward with Fremont

To Morris, Ruth, Joe and Jonathan

Contents

■ *Solomon Carvalho Joins Fremont*

    1   Invitation to Adventure 3
    2   A Way for the Lord 7
    3   Farewell to Friends 12
    4   Packing for the Journey 19

■ *Westward from St. Louis*

    5   St. Louis, September 14, 1853 31
    6   Preparing for the Trail 36
    7   Solomon Carvalho, Great Medicine
          Man 46
    8   Solomon Carvalho, M.D. 52
    9   The Great Divide 58
  10   New Year's Day, 1854 64

■ *Hardships of the Trail*

  11   On Guard 75
  12   The Oath 83
  13   Lost in the Snows 90
  14   Licked! 97

15 Put Not Your Trust in Princes 104
16 Parowan 112
17 Salt Lake City 116
18 War or Peace? 122
19 The Hated Hornadoes 129

■ *After the Adventure*

20 All Israel is Responsible for
    One Another 137
21 The Charter 143
22 Mr. Solomon Nunes Carvalho,
    Author 148
23 Free Soil, Free Speech, and
    Fremont 153
24 Looking Backward 160

Solomon Carvalho Joins Fremont

1 *Invitation to Adventure*

"I give you my solemn word, sir. You may expect me at St. Louis on the fourteenth day of September."

Solomon Carvalho could scarcely believe that the words sounding in his ears were his own. Perhaps it was some sort of madness. In the course of half an hour he had left the world of reality and had entered a world known to him only in his most romantic dreams. One half hour with the magnificent man before him had changed him from an ordinary citizen of Baltimore into a man of action—a builder of the United States of America. In this rosy dream, Solomon saw his businessman's suit change into a frontiersman's leather jerkin and his prosaic hat become a fur cap.

This was the new Solomon Carvalho, member-to-be

of Fremont's party of exploration, encountering his destiny as empire builder. The dreamer became a doer, with a mountain staff in one hand and a camera in the other, striding over the lofty Rocky Mountains, following John Charles Fremont, pathfinder of trails, over the continent as far as the great Pacific Ocean.

All this was for the future. Solomon came back to the present with a jolt. What would his wife, Sarah, say when he told her of his decision? And what of his young children?

But Colonel Fremont was talking again.

"Mr. Carvalho, you have shown complete understanding of the purpose of this expedition. You can do so much for it. As I have pointed out, you will be the first photographer who has ever gone on a journey of exploration of any kind. Your pictures will prove to the world in general, and to Jefferson Davis in particular, that the route for the new railroad should be the one that my fourth expedition has already used. The 38th parallel of latitude is the route the American people must use for opening up the new West."

Shaking his head impatiently, the Colonel continued: "It would be a tragedy for the American people if the railroad were built through Texas simply because Congress wished to win favor with that state and other slave-holding states."

Solomon silently applauded his words. Fremont was a leader who knew how to appeal to the fighting instinct of a man. He had thrown out a challenge. Here was a good cause to fight for—for a free America against the forces of slavery, the burning issue of the times.

"Fight" was the correct word, because the journey would be a fight against nature itself. It would be a tough march over hard country where white men had scarcely trod before. They would experience severe weather and cold as bitter as that of the arctic regions. It was not to be a trip in covered wagons over roads already marked out. There would only be the faintest trace of a trail. The Colonel explained frankly that he had deliberately chosen the winter season for his trip as this would prove to all that the route over the 38th parallel could serve as an all-weather road for the railway then being planned to link the two oceans.

Solomon rose to leave. The Colonel stood up too. The guest was surprised. He had thought that this heroic man would tower over him. Instead, he was able to look directly into his eyes. They were both of the same height and build. Power, then, does not lie in superior stature. Solomon felt more sure than ever that he could and would be at St. Louis on the fourteenth day of September.

He hastened to say good-bye to the man who had changed the course and quality of his life. He hurried because he felt that every minute counted in the preparation. Between the twenty-second of August, the day of his meeting with the Pathmaker, and the day of their rendezvous in St. Louis only three weeks remained, and he was determined to get ready with no loss of time.

Mrs. Jessie Benton Fremont saw him to the door and shook hands with him on leaving. Hurrying down C Street he thought of the Colonel's lady. What a study she would make for a daguerreotype! With her wide eyes and her classic nose and strong chin, her dark hair parted in the middle and her simple dress of a violet-colored muslin with the one white flower at her belt, she was fit to grace the White House. She looked like a lady. But more than that—she showed courage.

What other woman would have allowed her husband to spend half his married life away from her on his trips into the Far West? Would Sarah be ready to do the same? It would only be for a year or less and it would be the chance of a lifetime. Solomon began to line up the arguments he would use to plead his case.

He stepped into the stagecoach which would return him to the city of Baltimore. He was determined that this chance for fame would be worth fighting for, even if his wife offered some resistance.

2 *A Way for the Lord*

"Nachamu, nachamu, ami."

" 'Be comforted, be comforted, my people,' said the Lord."

The voice of Solomon Nunes Carvalho rang out confidently from the reader's desk of the Har Sinai Synagogue. The congregation settled back in their oaken pews, prepared to enjoy the Sabbath portion. With his knowledge of Hebrew and his tuneful voice, Solomon was well equipped to chant the words of the Prophet Isaiah.

Mr. Carvalho often assumed this task, substituting for the Cantor. But today the place of honor had been given to him in special recognition. For he was now a national figure whose name had appeared in the newspapers of America. As a member of the congregation, Solomon had brought fame to the Jews of

Baltimore and honor to Jews everywhere. The name of Solomon Nunes Carvalho would be on the lips of every red-blooded American and especially if that American was of the Jewish faith. Before the week was over, Carvalho would set forth to cut his way through the width of an immense continent. He would be making history as a member of the expedition led by Colonel John Charles Fremont. Much time would elapse before this congregation of the people of Baltimore would again enjoy Solomon's presence at Sabbath service.

The Cantor settled himself in his seat behind the reader, listening to the message of the Prophet. This week had seen the observance of the Ninth Day of Av in the Jewish calendar, the tragic day on which the Temple in Jerusalem had twice been destroyed. True to the Jewish tradition never to lose hope, the Prophet speaks out, bringing a promise in the name of the Lord of better times in the future of the Jewish people.

The sun broke through the low morning clouds and brought a cheerful light through the windows of the somber synagogue. The beautiful words of the Prophet continued. To the listeners the words seemed symbolic of the journey that lay before the company of adventurers:

"The voice of him that crieth in the wilderness: 'Prepare a way for the Lord; make straight through the desert a highway for the Lord; every valley shall be raised and every mountain shall be leveled.' "

Imagination visualized those mountains and deserts. Fantastic as it might seem, Carvalho would have to traverse them. To say that the mountains were two or three miles high was no exaggeration. Pike's Peak, for instance, was known to be close to fifteen thousand feet high—and it was not the highest elevation in the tremendous range which ran like a spine down the length of the continent. Like an immense fence, the Rocky Mountains stood there, a tremendous barrier preventing the crossing to the Pacific Ocean.

And as for the deserts, one of them was called Death Valley—and with good reason.

For weeks the newspapers had been full of the accounts of the four previous journeys of Colonel Fremont. They seemed like adventure stories which could exist only in the imagination of a writer of fiction. Often the accounts of danger made the readers shudder in fright.

What a coincidence that the Bible portion of the week told about it so certainly! It was like a prophecy of things to come. The words of the Prophet Isaiah rose from the lectern and seemed as fresh and real as the day they had been spoken twenty-five hundred years before.

In the women's gallery, Mrs. Carvalho sat with folded hands, her eyes down-bent on her Bible. The text was familiar to her; she had spent considerable time teaching the religion of her people to the youth of Baltimore. The words flowing through her eyes and ears gave her strength.

She raised her eyes and looked down, first at her little son, David, sitting downstairs with the men in his father's seat, and then at her husband. At thirty-eight, Solomon was no longer a young man, but he certainly looked fit and healthy as he stood at the altar. Each month he had gone with his rifle company on hikes and so he was accustomed to the outdoors. But could he withstand the trials of a difficult journey? She remembered reading in the newspapers how even the Colonel, a man accustomed to the rigors of outdoor life, was to that day suffering and ill as a result of the cold and discomforts of his mountain journeys.

What makes a man go out into danger, knowing full well that the odds are against him? What makes him continue on in such an existence, where life often hangs by a thread?

And Mrs. Carvalho wondered about Jessie Fremont.

"Will she be in church praying that the God of all men take care of her husband, too?"

Mrs. Carvalho stopped her straying thoughts. Solomon stood in the pulpit—handsome and dark—almost like the Prophet Isaiah himself. Colonel Fremont, she was told, was dark and handsome like her husband. His straight nose and strong, determined chin resembled those of her Solomon. Both were men of action, although their eyes had the dreamy look of men of vision. Each would drive himself to struggle against odds to fulfill his purpose.

Mrs. Carvalho sighed. She was proud of her husband. Until this time, his life had been unexciting, taken up with his business and with the Jewish community in which he lived. She had been surprised and shocked when he told her of his promise to the Colonel. But how could she stand in his way when he seemed so determined?

The reading of the Law over, Solomon invoked the blessing in a firm tone. Then he joined in the traditional procession which returned the Scroll to the Ark. He resumed his seat near his son, just behind the oak railing.

Rabbi Moritz Brown mounted the pulpit and concluded the Sabbath morning prayers. He recited the Adoration prayer and the new prayer for the welfare of the American government and its president. He raised his arms in the priestly blessing.

Following the services, the congregants clustered around the table in the social hall for the blessings over the wine and bread. Then they sat down in groups at the tables decked with white tablecloths for the Sabbath, to enjoy a leisurely visit with their Jewish neighbors.

3 *Farewell to Friends*

Baltimore, with its fifteen hundred Jews, was the second largest Jewish community in the United States. It had no less than three synagogues, because the Jewish population was spread along the Patapsco River of the Chesapeake Bay. From the synagogue on Bolton Street, some of them would have to walk at least one mile to get to their homes. Saturday was an opportunity to visit with friends from all over the far-flung city and to enjoy the companionship of people of their own religion. This pleasure would not come again until the following Sabbath.

On this day in 1853, the topic of conversation between friends ordinarily might have been the problem facing all Americans at this time. Slavery was dividing the nation and it was plain to see that the question was increasing in seriousness.

Today, however, the conversation turned immediately to the startling news about Carvalho. The hall was filled with eager voices. Suddenly in one of the lulls which come in any gathering, everyone heard:

"But in the dead of winter!"

It was the voice of Rosa Abulafia—not any louder than usual—which carried over to the other side of the social room for all to hear. After she had made the remark, Rosa realized the stillness. She looked around and blushed. Rosa was shy. Of a very pious nature, she was gentle from the tips of her Sabbath gloves to the little feathered red hat which she wore on her white hair. Rosa blushed again, redder than before.

She remained silent, wishing that she were somewhere else or that she could say something clever to take away from the awkward thing she had just said. The little music teacher sat as still as when she had had her daguerreotype taken. Just so had she sat in her Empire dress of gray with its high waist and puffed sleeves. Solomon Carvalho smiled and crossed to Rosa. She smiled timidly as she raised her eyes to him.

"That's just why," he said. "That's why, Miss Rosa. The Colonel is anxious to prove that these Rocky Mountains can be crossed. . . ."

He stopped and quickly changed the words he was about to use.

"The Colonel is anxious to prove to everyone

that these Rocky Mountains can be crossed even when the snow lies deepest."

David Nunes broke in.

"Well, if anyone can do it, Colonel Fremont can. This will be his . . . is it his fourth trip?"

His brother corrected him.

"No, this is to be his fifth. His fourth was when he crossed over to California and afterward became its senator."

"California," sighed Rosa Abulafia, who had now recovered from her embarrassment. "Lovely ladies . . . a land of sunshine and singing . . . a picture of romance. Dancing . . . colored skirts twirling . . . black hair piled up high with brilliant combs. The clicking of heels in the Spanish fandango with the sound of castanets."

Her aged mother sighed too.

"It's not the fandango I'm thinking of. It's my rheumatism that worries me. August is not over and already I begin to dread the long Maryland winters. If it isn't the cold or the sniffles it's something more serious like pneumonia. And bringing the coal to keep the fires burning and then carrying the ashes out afterward. . . ."

This time again Solomon came to the rescue. Old Mrs. Leah Abulafia was known as a constant complainer. Some of the Jewish community had given her the nickname of "the Mrs. Gummidge of Baltimore." This was because she reminded them of the character in a book by Charles Dickens, the English writer who was being read by many Americans.

Solomon said, "I assure you I will bring you some of that old Spanish California sunshine when I return. What kind would you like? They say that the California mission wine is equal to any we buy from Spain itself."

In the laugh that broke the tension, Rosa collected her mother's cup with her own and returned them to the table. A slow walk would take them back to their brick house fronting Bolton Street.

Soon afterward, most of the Sabbath worshipers rose from their seats to return home for the Sabbath nap that would follow a leisurely meal. In their imaginations, they could smell the Sabbath stew known as *chond* which contained lamb and a little bit of every kind of vegetable cooked over a slow flame. Its taste and inviting smell seemed to embody the very spirit of the Sabbath itself.

Solomon stayed on with the Rabbi. His mind was excited at the thought of the impending trip.

Solomon liked to talk. He had interesting friends among men of his own profession. With these artists and photographers he would discuss the new trends in their calling. Solomon was an artist in his own right. In the social hall behind him was his picture of Moses receiving the tablets of the Law on Mt. Sinai —a picture that had gained him a prize in a national contest.

Rabbi Brown reached for a piece of honey-cake. His lips moved in the blessing: "Blessed art Thou, King of the Universe, who hast created the various grains."

Then, having bitten into the cake, he turned to his friend and congregant.

"We will miss you, Solomon. We will miss your help in the community, and we will miss your friendship. I do want to congratulate you on your reading today."

Solomon said, "For this you can thank my father who taught me."

"Yes," replied Rabbi Brown. "When your father was judge, his knowledge of the Talmud helped him to give just verdicts. He tried to follow in the footsteps of Moses, our teacher, by giving judgments that were right and proper."

Solomon concurred. "Mother always said that twenty-four hours in the day was not enough for him. He was a great scholar and he wrote a translation of the Psalms."

Little David standing by was not interested in the Psalms.

"Didn't Grandfather fight?" he asked.

"Yes," said his father. "When he was young he fought the British and helped defend Charleston."

Rabbi Brown asked a question.

"I have been curious. How did Colonel Fremont get your name?"

Solomon laughed. "I don't know and I didn't

have the time to ask him. There were so many details we had to discuss. However, I'm glad that the Colonel heard of me and sent for me. I thank my stars he didn't invite Mathew Brady or I know that Mathew would have accepted. Even though we are good friends, I am afraid that Mathew will be jealous of me."

"You have earned the invitation. You have a good reputation in your chosen work. You mustn't be so modest."

Solomon's laugh rang through the empty hall.

"You are most kind, Rabbi. There are not many people who would agree with you. I am not modest. But I do believe that as Americans we should go out and help build our magnificent country. You have always encouraged us to do so."

Rabbi Brown was pleased.

"In that you are correct. You were born in this country. So you do not know, as I do, what the Jew has had to suffer in many parts of Europe. Your father, too, came from a land which has been good to the Jews. England is known for its treatment of minority people. But I come from Central Europe and can tell you tales of the trouble which our people have had to bear at the hands of ignorant, bigoted men. Please God, David will never have to see this sort of thing in the United States."

Solomon Nunes Carvalho nodded his head slowly.

"The Sefardi Jew was the first to come to this land and has had a proud history here since Asser Levy came to New Amsterdam at the time of the Dutch. Now," and Solomon stood up to his full stature, "now please God, another Sefardi Jew will help to make history. The first photographer to enlarge the boundaries of our land! It will be a Sefardi Jew who will find a way through the Rockies for the steam engines which will carry people into the Californias to settle the land which the Colonel took for America."

Both Rabbi Brown and Solomon would have liked to continue their conversation. The rabbi was always ready to listen to stories of the greatness of this land which had just added another state to its frontiers. But the caretaker who looked after the synagogue was waiting to close up and besides Solomon had promised his wife that he would be back for the Sabbath meal.

The Rabbi could not resist a joke.

"You are bringing Leah a bottle of California wine. What will you bring me?"

Solomon gave a final glance around the large and friendly community hall. He let the Rabbi go out first as he said, "I will bring you pure olive oil for the eternal lamp."

"Bring me an Indian, Daddy," said David not to be left out.

4 *Packing for the Journey*

Little David Carvalho watched as his father packed for the journey. Father had often gone off into the country before on trips. But this was to be different. From the expression on Mother's face, this absence would be for more than just a week, and David clung to his father. Even a boy of five was not too young to understand the seriousness of the journey and the separation it would bring.

His father's stoutest boots went into the bundle. They looked strong enough to last a long time.

"What are these?" asked David as his father put away some packets. David knew his letters and he spelled out "A-L-D-E-N" from the side of the tins.

"That says Alden," said his father. Mr. Alden sells these tins. This is coffee and this is cocoa and these are milk and eggs and cream."

David was puzzled.

"They don't look like eggs or milk or cream to me," he said.

"No," laughed his father. "This is something new. It is called powdered or preserved food. It has been dried and packed away in packages so that it can be carried a long distance. When you mix it with water, you get food which tastes like the original thing. Mr. Alden wants us to try his invention to see if it is worthwhile."

"But," said David, "why couldn't you buy these things in a store? Mother sends Hattie to the store and the grocery man sends some things in his cart."

His father explained.

"You see, David," he answered, "we will be passing through country where there will be no stores and no shops. We will have to depend on ourselves for food."

"Will you be shooting the food you need?" asked David. "Will you be shooting buffalo and deer and rabbits?"

His father nodded.

"That is exactly what we will be doing. We will be hunting for our food and fishing in the streams for our fish."

Mrs. Carvalho passed by the open door as these words were spoken. She and her husband were practicing Jews. In their home she served only those meats which had been killed according to Jewish ritual. These she took home from the butcher and carefully soaked and salted, a process which took an hour and a half. On this trip her husband would have to forget these rules for there would be no way of observing them.

David wasn't interested in rules of the kitchen. He was excited about the idea of shooting buffalo and deer.

"Will you take me?" he begged his dad for the thousandth time. He thought that if he asked often enough, he might wear down his father's resistance.

"Not this time," said his father gently.

Already, another basket was being packed. His father began to put away his daguerreotype materials. David was familiar with these items. There were the slides, each in a frame of wood, and there were the mysterious bottles of chemicals. He recognized the color and the smell of each one.

The mercury fascinated the little boy most. It was silvery and Father would roll some out of the bottle into the palm of his hand. David would have to watch it carefully or it would roll to the floor. If you let it drop to the floor, it would break up into little balls which would slide about on the floor. Then you would try to pick them up and put them together again in a bigger ball or you would try to pick them up with a cardboard. Sometimes David's father played a trick on him and covered David's lead soldiers with the mercury. It had another name —quicksilver—and the name suited it very well. It was quick and it turned everything silver.

Father sniffed at the white liquid in another bottle. That was the alcohol. It smelled like wine or whisky but Father said it was bad to drink. It could make you very sick. Father handled his precious chemicals very carefully, especially the iodine that could make a mess with its purple color.

David felt very proud of his father. Father was an artist and a daguerreotyper. He could take your picture in two ways. You could come to his studio and he would paint your picture on a big canvas, patiently putting on the colors with a brush as he talked to you. Then you got a very good big picture which you could frame and hang on the wall over your piano at home. Or, you could get your picture done very quickly by a new method called daguerreotypy. You sat in a chair, very still, in just the position that Father arranged. When he was satisfied, his head would disappear behind a black cloth. You could see the rest of his body and his hand holding the rubber ball.

"Smile, please," said Father as he pressed the bulb that made the shutter click. Father would then take out the slide and carry it to the back room. There he would treat it with all sorts of chemicals. Then he would come back, before the ladies had their gloves on, with a very lovely little picture.

David often wondered about these new chemicals. His father said that chemistry would do wonderful things for America some day.

The Free Library of Philadelphia

The thought suddenly came to David: "Where will you develop your plates?"

His mind was quick to see the difficulties which could face the photographer in the open. Solomon was pleased with his son's intelligence.

"Well, David," he said, "this will be real pioneering. We are trying for the first time to do something which has never been done before. And I have taken along some chemicals which will be special for cold weather."

Mrs. Carvalho came into the room with the baby in her arms.

"My brother has come from Philadelphia," she said.

Emanuel Solis followed on her footsteps with his quick bustling stride.

"Solomon," he explained, "I had to come. I found an excuse and told Esther that I had business in Baltimore."

He bent over and patted David's cheeks. "How are you, David?" he said.

Emanuel lost no time in stating his business. He was the elder brother of Sarah and considered himself the person responsible for the well-being of the family. He had looked with ill-favor on the match between his sister and the proud Carvalho. There was no denying that the Carvalho family was a respectable and distinguished one, but Solomon had never stuck to one thing for a long time. Too bad that he had not settled down in the teaching profession. It would have been better if he had chosen something steady.

Sarah was not the complaining kind but he knew that his sister often had to practice careful habits in housekeeping in order to make the money last. An artist could not really make a good living for his wife. Even the new daguerreotype business failed to bring in enough for a Solis daughter to manage on.

And now to make matters worse, Solomon was going off to be killed. It was his duty to change the mind of this stubborn man who had become his brother-in-law. Yet he must do so in a way that would not make him angry.

Solomon sensed that this visit might not be a pleasant one. He turned to his son.

"David, will you go to the kitchen and tell Hattie that we have a guest and that we would like some of those delicious cookies we smelled in the baking this morning and also a pot of coffee that she makes so well."

David hurried off to deliver the message.

"It is good of you to come," said Carvalho, turning to his guest.

Emanuel burst out, "I suppose there is nothing I can say to make you change your mind?"

"What do you mean?"

"What do you mean what do I mean?" exploded Emanuel. "Why do you ask 'what do you mean?' I'll tell you what I mean. Listen to this." And he took from his inside pocket a folded newspaper. "Listen to what the *Baltimore Sun* says. I'm reading from the paper of three days ago. Listen to this and you will see what I mean. 'Suffering privation, the unhappy expedition suffered torture of desert heat and mountain cold; Indian treachery awaited them. The men of the party suffered starvation in the Rockies. They were reduced to eating their own animals. In the end, Fremont, Pruese, Godey and Saunders reached the Red River Settlement after ten days' agonizing struggle on starvation rations. The rescue party found twenty-three remaining men, tottering skeletons, with bloodless faces, who cried like children as they were lifted onto the mules and taken to camp at Taos.' "

"Are you finished, Emanuel?" asked Solomon. "That is the story that is being given to the public. But what are the facts, the actual facts? Don't think that I didn't follow the progress of the fourth expedition Fremont led across the Rockies. Everyone makes mistakes. Fremont made a mistake then. He hired and listened to the advice of an old trapper whom he liked. Williams was his name. Bill Williams. Bill had spent some twenty-five years of his life trapping in various parts of the Rocky Mountains. Who would have thought that this man, experienced as he was, would have made such a mistake?"

Solomon seemed to be quite another man and not the little daguerreotyper of Eutaw Street. He seemed to be six feet tall and the bottle flashed like a sword in his hand.

"True, we are going on a dangerous expedition. True, I entered this venture on an impulse. True, I did not ask Sarah her feelings on the matter. But I have passed my word to Colonel Fremont that I will go on this trip and the Colonel did not hide anything from me. He pointed out that there would be danger to face. And I know no other man that I would trust with my life under similar circumstances."

Emanuel listened in astonished silence.

Solomon went on.

"Colonel Fremont's extraordinary contribution to the study of astronomy and geography has interested me for a long time. This is not a man who lets his heart run away with his head. Whatever he sets out to do, he finishes. Granted that men have died and will continue to die. But that is the only way that our country can be built, and I, for one, am determined that I will not turn back at this point."

David, carrying the cookies, stood in the doorway. His wondering eyes took in the flushed cheeks of his father and the offended look of his uncle.

Solomon turned decisively to Emanuel.

"I thank you for coming. Wish me 'derech Tz'lechah.' What the Lord has in mind will most certainly come true. We will, with the grace of God, find our way through the Rockies. We will, by the grace of God, return with the pictures which will prove to the whole world that the continent can be spanned by a railroad and furthermore that this rail-road can function in all weathers."

Emanuel saw in the face of his in-law the expression of either a madman or a prophet. He could not tell which. In the face of such strength and determination, he could not hope to make headway. He spoke in a calm voice.

"*Tsay b'shalom*," he said. "Go in peace and return to the bosom of your family in peace. Bring honor to yourself and to your family and to all Israel."

Westward from St. Louis

5 *St. Louis,*
September 14, 1853

It was September 12, and Solomon had managed to make good time. He was congratulating himself. Seven days from New York to St. Louis was a very good record for this distance and Solomon was certain that he would meet the deadline. He had enjoyed the trip on the steamboat and expected that less than a day would bring them to St. Louis, Missouri.

At the village of Alton a disappointment awaited Solomon and the rest of the passengers. When the boat was tied up, the captain assembled all the passengers in the salon and told them the bad news. He hoped that they would understand and forgive. Since the water in the Illinois River was so shallow, the boat would be unable to proceed and all passengers would have to disembark. However, there was some comfort and the situation was not hopeless. A stagecoach company there would take care of those who wanted to go on to St. Louis.

Solomon had no difficulty in getting a place on the coach for the next morning. He hoped that there would be no more delays and that he would be on time for the meeting with the Colonel.

On the next morning, Carvalho was watching the loading of his precious baskets to the top of the coach to make sure they were being handled properly when the manager of the company came along and asked whose baskets these were. Solomon said they were his.

"In that case," said the man, "you will have to have them sent on the next coach. As you can see, this is an emergency and we have had to accommodate more passengers than we had planned for."

Solomon showed his disappointment.

"I do not know how I can keep my appointment with the Colonel," he said to the passengers who came up to commiserate with him. "And I will not leave my baskets behind. I must have them under my care at all times."

The manager of the stagecoach, busy at supervising the loading of the baggage, was able to overhear the conversation. At the words "the Colonel" he plucked up his ears and turned to Mr. Carvalho.

"Excuse me, sir," he said. "Did you say the Colonel? Were you referring to *the* Colonel?"

"Well," said Solomon, "if you are thinking of Colonel Fremont, you are right. I am on my way to join his expedition. We are to meet in St. Louis on the fourteenth day of September. In those baskets are the cameras and plates which I will need to photograph the trip."

The stagecoach manager swung around and shouted to someone in the stables.

"Eb, harness up two more horses and hitch them to the stage. And you, Bill, get these baskets up on top. This gentleman is on his way to join the Colonel's party to the West."

Then, turning to Solomon he said, "I was with the Colonel on his first trip to Oregon country. I wish you good luck. You will never find a man like him. He is the most noble specimen I have ever set eyes on. Wish I were going with you."

Solomon put out his hand with the money for the extra baggage but the man refused to take it. He said, "I will not take this money. Anything to help the Colonel. Only wish I were going," he added again.

Solomon reached St. Louis within the few hours. He had kept his promise. Round him was the excitement of a frontier city. It was bubbling with activity. On the streets East and West seemed to meet elbow to elbow. Senators from Washington rubbed shoulders with frontiersmen dressed in moccasins and leather jackets. Here was the jumping-off place for the Far West.

The Colonel was waiting impatiently for him at the home of Colonel Brant. He was eager to be off. A ticket for a berth on a river steamer to Kansas City was handed to the photographer. On the boat, Solomon was to meet several men of his party, among them one Mr. Bomar, a photographer.

Solomon wondered why Mr. Bomar seemed less friendly than the engineers Egloffstein and Fuller. The answer to the question in Solomon's mind came on their arrival in Kansas City. The Colonel asked the two photographers to try their skills. As an experiment each one was to take a picture of the scene from the hotel window.

As Solomon told his colleagues afterward, it was a triumph for the copperplate picture. Solomon had only to take the picture and then wash the plate in his chemicals. The wax paper process that Bomar used required changing the negative to a positive and this took twelve hours.

"Could you see the Colonel holding up his men for twelve hours every time he wanted a picture?" Solomon would chuckle.

The Colonel called Solomon on the next morning.

"Well, Mr. Carvalho, this leaves only you as our official photographer. Now you must decide. Do you have any doubts about this trip? Standing close to the frontier as you do now, you are in a better position to realize the dangers and discomforts which face us. If you desire to step out, there will be no loss to you. I will be glad, of course, to repay you for your time and for the expenses you have had. What is your answer? You need not give it to me now. Tomorrow will be time enough."

Solomon had his answer ready.

"At what time do we start, sir?"

The Colonel was touched.

"Thank you, Mr. Carvalho," he said.

6 *Preparing for the Trail*

The Delaware Indians who joined the Fremont expedition were a magnificent group of men. Like their leader, Captain Wolff, they were six feet tall and powerful. Like their leader they were all chiefs in their tribes.

Solomon's real friendship with their leader began when they were camped at Westport near Kansas City while they were preparing for the trip and buying their equipment and animals.

Captain Wolff was sick and was being treated by a medicine man. Solomon watched the medicine man at work. Wolff was put into a lodge only high enough for him to sit. He was naked and he was doubled up with pain. From behind the flap of the tent, the medicine man handed Wolff a pipe which the sick man had to smoke until the lodge was filled with smoke. The medicine man stood just outside the lodge, reciting words of magic. Poor Captain Wolff was almost suffocated by the time the medicine man decided that it was time to move the patient. Wrapped in a blanket, he was carried to his own tent, where Solomon found him an hour later, with an intense headache and pains in his back.

Solomon asked Wolff whether he would be willing to try some of his medicine. To this Wolff agreed, so Solomon gave him some calomel tea. With this white powder, Solomon gave him a spoonful of Epsom salts. When Solomon returned in an hour, Wolff said that he felt altogether well and that his pains had gone. Solomon followed up his treatment with some pudding which he made with arrowroot. This was a pleasant way of giving the patient food which was easily digested. By morning, Wolff was well. He had had a stomach disorder. He would certainly have died if the medicine man had given him any more of his "treatments."

That evening, round the campfire, Solomon wished to give the men a treat and thought of the cognac in his medicine chest. This cognac had taken on a slightly black color but was still tasty. When Solomon went to get it, he found that the bottle had disappeared. There was only one bottle left—some whisky which contained a chemical which the daguerreotyper had added to be used for his plates.

The chemical had turned the whisky black. While Solomon stood looking at this second bottle, an idea came to him.

He went back to the campfire and said he was sorry that he could not find the cognac and that they would not be able to make the toast after all. He told them that the bottle which was left was needed for his craft. He said that the bottle which had been taken contained a chemical which would kill in forty-eight hours anyone who was foolish enough to drink enough of it. While speaking Solomon eyed one of the mule drivers who seemed to be slightly drunk.

The next morning Solomon found that the bottle of cognac had been returned to the chest though it was half empty. The whole episode was a good joke, but Solomon could not share it with anyone in camp.

Another event which he did not share with the men happened on the following day. A prairie fire was raging all round the camp. The camp itself was safe as it was surrounded by a river on three sides and the fourth was a good distance from the fire.

Carvalho was curious to see the fire at closer range so he rode out alone to get a good look at it. Unfortunately he lost his direction and had a hard time getting back to the camp. It took him three hours to circle the river and to blunder into the camp. Solomon felt foolish and told no one about the experience.

Hardships of this kind were valuable in changing

Solomon from a city-dweller to a man accustomed to
the constant dangers he would have to face in the
wilderness. At Salt Creek, a little further along the
trail, a heavy storm came up with rain and sleet. In
the middle of the night their tent was torn down.
The men attempted to raise it again but were unable to do so as the tent pins would not hold in the
soggy ground. There was nothing they could do but
huddle under their waterproof blankets until morning when they dried themselves around a fire and
then searched for their belongings which had been
carried away by the strong wind. Their animals had
broken their tethers and had scattered to the woods
for shelter under the trees. Fortunately, the men
were able to recover them all.

Solomon was now more than ever determined that
he would do his best to perform his share of the
duties of the expedition successfully.

When they reached Westport, which was their
first campsite, he had occasion to notice that the baskets were standing up poorly under the rough treatment they received. He realized that if his cameras
were not to be smashed to bits, he must find cases for
them. At the first opportunity, when they were
camped at a village near the principal town of the
Pottawatomies, he sought out a blacksmith shop.
The blacksmith was away but his wife gave Solomon
permission to use his tools. Solomon had brought a
large supply of wood packing cases which he had
found in camp.

He set to work with saw and hatchet and using the blacksmith's nails, made up some very tough boxes. Over the lumber he stretched some rawhide which was in the shop. When the blacksmith returned, Solomon paid him five dollars for the materials which he had used.

Solomon was certain that the mule drivers would be pleased with these sturdy boxes. However, they did not look forward to packing and unpacking these cases and blamed Carvalho for the added work. When they brought their complaints to the Colonel they were told that this was an important part of the work of the expedition.

The Colonel's blunt words angered the drivers. They deliberately tried to displease Solomon. He had to be on the alert after that, as the muleteers would frequently load and pack very carelessly. On more than one occasion, Solomon found the buffing brush lying on the trail. Once he found that the keg of alcohol was missing. When the Colonel sent a man back to look, the keg was found half empty.

On the Republican River, Solomon discovered that camping was republican in the real sense of the word. Every man was equal and everyone had to take care of himself. Solomon approached some of the muleteers to do some washing for him as he was in need of fresh linens. One after the other they refused, so Solomon had to get some soap from the Quartermaster and go down to the Republican River where he rubbed away his knuckles but returned

with clean clothes. By spreading them on the grass to dry and then under his couch beneath the rubber blanket, he managed to have some well-pressed apparel.

For those who were good with their fingers, there was another job in camp-housekeeping—making moccasins and buckskin mittens. Solomon proved very adept at this skill.

Another preparation, which seemed more manly, was perfecting one's skill in shooting. Solomon became a proficient marksman, hitting the bull's-eye three times out of five.

He was able to put this skill to good use when he was invited to a buffalo hunt. It all began because Wolff said to Solomon, "What for you no hunt? Plenty buffalo here. Got buffalo pongo."

This last was in reference to the horse which had been assigned to Solomon. It had been trained by the Indians for buffalo hunting and was adept at stepping aside when the buffalo lunged at the rider.

So the next day, when the Indians saw signs of "plenty cow," the whole camp went out. Solomon chased his prey for five miles, not knowing that the Indian method was to stand up in the stirrups and shoot directly from the saddle. By the time Solomon had caught up to his bull, the rest of his comrades were miles away.

Solomon did bring down his bull with several shots, finally killing it with his pistol. The buffalo

The Free Library of Philadelphia

fell, but by this time, Solomon was parted from his comrades.

Solomon found himself alone on the prairie. What's more, he had left his compass at camp and could not find his way. A trip to the top of a hill helped him locate Smokey Hill about twenty miles away. Solomon rested his horse for a while and then set his horse in the direction of the village.

On the way he came upon Welachus, a Delaware Indian of the camp party. He was looking for the tomahawk which he had lost during the buffalo hunt. It was fortunate for Solomon that he met Welachus because he was six points off the correct course to the camp.

Around the campfire afterward, the Indians would not believe that Carvalho had actually brought down a bull. He described how he did it and even said that he had chosen a cow thinking that the meat would be more tender, only to find out that he had shot a bull after all.

Captain Wolff said, "Sorry! Captain Wolff no believe. Captain Wolff shoot buffalo, he cut tongue to bring home. Carvalho no bring tongue. No kill buffalo."

Carvalho could not deny that he had not brought back any evidence. In his memory he saw again the look in the eyes of the bull as he sank down on the prairie. It was a look of such sadness that Solomon tried not to remember at all.

7 *Solomon Carvalho,*
Great Medicine Man

The Cheyenne and Pawnee Indians were at war
with each other. The Fremont party crossing the
Great Plains, watered by the Arkansas River, was
camping at Big Timber, a Cheyenne village in Colorado of about two hundred lodges and with about a
thousand people.

For Solomon, these people were fascinating. And
since he was a "medicine man," he was in a position
to see every phase of the life of the Indians of the
village.

An immense fire was burning in the center of the
village. Women, dressed in wolf skins, were beating
drums and howling and chanting. Round the fire,
the braves, dressed in hideous war paint and wearing

giant feather headdresses, helped the women make the night even more horrible with their wild cries.

The scalps of the enemy had been mounted on a pole. One could tell they were Pawnees, as their heads were all shaved except for the scalp lock which had been stiffened with grease and looked like a horn. Solomon counted fifteen of these Pawnee scalps.

Mr. Egloffstein, a lover of music, was busy writing down the music of the Indians. It was funny to hear his description of the music. He was using modern musical terms to describe a primitive form.

"Listen!" he was saying. "There is always just the one key. Every song is sung in the same key and they never try to sing in harmony."

It was entirely different kind of camp that Carvalho saw on the following day. Everything was as quiet as a Sunday in Baltimore.

The Indians came out of their tepees to welcome Solomon. He had the magic which they loved. He could strike a little stick that had some blue substance at its end and out would come fire. He could use "firewater" to heat the chemicals which would send up a dense and mysterious vapor. He could take any article, dip it into a thick silvery liquid and the color of the object would change to silver. Of course the Indians had no way of knowing that the matches or iodine fumes or mercury were not magic but real chemicals from the outside world that were fast changing the life of men.

But best of all was to be invited by this strange

white medicine man to sit very quietly in the spot he would indicate and in the position he would choose for you. Then he would disappear behind the little black box so that you could see only the top of his head. He would study something in the magic black box which was mounted on three sticks. Sometimes he would come out and change the position of the sitter. Then he would take a square frame out of one box and put it into the front of the magic black box. He would pull out a shutter and then motion to the sitter not to move at all. By the time you counted three, he would remove the first little frame and perhaps put in another.

You could watch him place these frames one at a time on a rack under which there was a lamp which burned a blue flame. It smelled like firewater and from it a horrible smoke came out that made you cough. Then he would put the frame in a pan holding some liquid and tilt the pan carefully back and forth till all parts of the plate had been wetted.

Finally, when he seemed satisfied, the white man would wash the whole thing in clear water from the brook, and put it behind glass. It was unbelievable. There in front of you was the exact image of the person who had been sitting in front of the white medicine man.

Solomon made some fine daguerreotypes of the chief and his braves and also of the women of the village. Old and young, Solomon photographed them.

There was the proud Indian chief in his buffalo skin robes that showed he had been a successful hunter. There was the old woman, worn with work and dried by the wind and the hot sun. Though she was probably not more than forty years old, she had seen the best part of her life go by. Her wrinkled old hands were no longer capable of doing much more than tend the little baby by her side.

One picture Solomon liked especially was of the Indian princess. She was a beautiful girl. She came to be photographed in her costly robe, embroidered with elk's teeth, beads and porcupine quills. Her arms were almost entirely covered with bracelets of copper and brass. Silver was rare in this section of the country and she had one silver bracelet that she valued more than the rest.

After the sitting, Carvalho signaled for her to give him one of the copper bracelets. Then, taking it in one hand, and dipping it in the quicksilver, he made motions in the air, saying, "Presto, pass!"

When the girl looked again, she saw with surprise that the bracelet had turned a silver color. After that, it was easy to get the squaws to sit for their portraits.

The Cheyenne were handsome Indians. Carvalho showed their background as farmers of the plain. It was the Colonel who had proven that the land between the Missouri River and the Rockies was not a desert as had been thought previously, but fine land that would in time grow wheat where grass now grew in abundance.

Because Solomon was such a wise magic man, he was invited to visit with the chief in his lodge. He ate buffalo steaks and venison around the campfire. The smoke from the fire in the center of the tepee was supposed to leave by the hole in the top but most of it managed to find its way back into the lodge.

Around the fire, the women had placed buffalo robes for the men to sit on. Back of them, against the walls of the lodge were the beds of cedar branches covered with hides and more fur robes. There was no furniture and the extra clothing was put under the bed.

Today the chief had a proposition for Solomon. It was nothing less than an invitation for Solomon to become a member of their tribe. He had such magic powers that they could use him as their medicine man.

Solomon graciously refused the honor. He told them that he had a wife at home far to the east and that his children would miss him. The chief assured Solomon that he could have another wife. He proposed that Solomon could choose for himself any of the girls of the camp as his second wife.

However, Solomon told him that he had given his solemn promise to the white captain that he would go on with him and that he could not break his promise. This was something that the Indians could understand. A promise was something sacred, not to be broken. The chief didn't coax Solomon any more after that.

Carvalho left the chief a fine knife as a gift and he received in return a fine bearskin. They parted with expressions of friendship.

8 *Solomon Carvalho, M.D.*

Carvalho liked the new title he had taken for himself—M.D. He laughed when the men asked him if he was also a doctor.

"No," said Carvalho. "M.D. stands for Mule Driver. Mule Driver Solomon Carvalho." He was proud of his title.

Carvalho enjoyed telling how one took care of a mule.

"First," he said, "you have to catch him."

And that was a job in itself. There, far away in the Huerfano Valley, is a speck among other specks. Animals feeding. Your eye picks out one particular mule that is your own. It is searching for a bit of grass to eat or the top of a bush to fill the empty feeling in its mule stomach.

The distance is a mile or perhaps more. Carvalho

has to tramp the snow. The mule lets him come within reaching distance but he has other plans. So, just as Solomon comes within a few yards of him, he dashes off. This happens many times. Looking out of the corner of his eye, he knows just when his master is too close for comfort. The only advantage Solomon has is the rope trailing from the mule. It is about thirty feet long. If only Solomon can get his hands on it, he has a sporting chance.

However, getting hold of the rope is not enough. The mule gallops off, pulling Solomon behind him. When Solomon has gotten this new treatment several times, his hands are not only frozen with the cold, but also burnt by the rope.

Solomon persists. Finally, he approaches the mule gently and stealthily, and succeeds in grabbing the rope securely. This time the mule stands still while Solomon mounts him bareback.

But getting on is no victory as Solomon soon learns. There is Solomon on the mule, coaxing and kicking and using the business end of the rope. But the animal cannot be persuaded to move. The mule's two front feet are planted in the snow as though they grew there.

Solomon is ready to give up in disgust. Fortunately one of the Delawares has been watching this little comedy and comes to help his friend. Washington, the Delaware, uses a great deal of persuasion in the form of kicks from the rear. This is the only kind of education that the mule knows and he wakes up from his dreams and gallops away, nearly shaking his master off. Every once in a while, the animal turns to look at his rider with a pleasant smile, showing his teeth as though he is enjoying the fun. He seems to be saying, "Don't you like this little game? It's all in fun, you know."

Solomon's answer is, "Stubborn mule."

In time, Solomon got to know the ways of a mule with a man and learned the tricks necessary to make the stubborn creature listen to the voice of his master. So he gave himself the title of "M.D." and felt that he deserved the great honor.

Not long afterward in the territory of the Ute Indians, Solomon received another title which the men gave him and which he earned for his ability to act. It was a long story and Solomon loved to tell it to any one who would listen.

It all began with a wild horse which the Delaware Indians found when they first entered Utah. Since it was fat and young and much juicier than the old horses they had been eating, they killed it and took the meat back to camp with them.

While they were seated round their campfire enjoying this meat, they were surprised to hear the loud voices of a very large crowd coming into the camp from the neighboring village. The spokesman was a Spanish half-breed. Solomon knew Spanish so he acted as interpreter. The village Indians said the horse being eaten really belonged to a squaw who stood near their spokesman. She claimed damages.

Carvalho took this message to the lodge where the Colonel sat. It was his policy never to come out to parley with the Indians directly. This made him important in the eyes of the Indians and also gave him time to think out very carefully what plan should be followed.

"In that case, Mr. Carvalho," said Fremont, "you must pay this woman for her horse."

The woman went back to her village, well satisfied with the red cloth, vermillion dye and blankets which she had received in payment for her horse.

"The story does not end here," Solomon would add with a chuckle.

On the next evening, when the men were enjoying an evening in the Colonel's lodge, their meal was interrupted again by the noise of a large party coming into the campsite.

When Solomon went out to see what was happening, he found a large crowd of Indians armed with rifles and bows and arrows and carrying powder horns and cartridge cases. They rode on fine horses and tried to impress the white men with their number and their strength.

They came to the point immediately. The horse which Captain Wolff had taken as food belonged to one of the members of their tribe. The man was demanding payment. Plenty of red cloth and blankets and dye and gunpowder. If the white men did not get them these things, they would fall upon them and take the goods.

Carvalho, much distressed, went back to tell the Colonel of the new development. Instead of being frightened, the Colonel laughed.

"Sir," said Solomon, "they are here in numbers and they have gunpowder and cartridges in their containers."

"Not at all," said the Colonel. "I know these people. If they had ammunition they would not be talking. We would all have been shot long ago. They are like children. They lie and bluff. Let us try something interesting. We will play their little game with them."

Then the Colonel laughed again.

"Now, Mr. Carvalho, are you a good actor?"

"Surely the Colonel must be joking," thought Carvalho, though this seemed hardly the time for jokes.

The Colonel tore a large sheet of paper from his diary and drew a circle on it.

"Now listen carefully," he said to Solomon and he spoke to him very earnestly for a few minutes. He seemed to be giving him directions.

Solomon walked out of the lodge and strode over to a large sycamore tree. Then he walked back about eighteen paces. Turning around, he fired one shot from his pistol, hitting the center. The Indians stopped in their tracks and pointed to their own guns as though to say, "That we can do, too."

Solomon paid no attention to them and fired another shot. This was new to the Indians. They had never seen a gun that could shoot twice without loading. Solomon stepped over to a young Indian brave and gave him the pistol, inviting him to shoot. The young man fired the gun and Solomon handed it to an old warrior, inviting him to do the same. Solomon kept this up until all six shots had been fired. While the last Indian was returning the gun to Solomon, he managed very quickly to exchange the pistol with the one in his belt. The second pistol, too, was passed around for the Indians to fire.

The Indians were convinced that the white men had magic guns that never needed reloading. They suddenly lost interest in their demands and began talking about trading. They spent some time trading goods and then requested Solomon to ask "the white captain" if they could spend the night in camp. When consulted, the Colonel said they could. However, he told the captain of the guard to make sure that there were special guards over the camp that night and especially over the horses.

Solomon and "the white captain" had a good laugh afterward. Solomon had carried out the directives of the Colonel and had put on a very convincing act. He later said that though he was a "bad actor," it had been "good medicine" for the Ute Indians.

9 *The Great Divide*

Solomon Carvalho, citizen of Baltimore, Maryland, photographer to John Charles Fremont's survey party, was standing on top of the world. The men had crossed the Huerfano River and were well into the Sangre de Cristo Range. Before him lay a fantastic sight. There was the Rio Grande River on its way through half a continent to the Gulf of Mexico. To his right was the Colorado plunging over mighty rocks to mingle finally with the waters of the Gulf of California. Behind him were the Platte and Arkansas rivers. It was the Arkansas River which they had followed to reach this spot. Together these two rivers would form the Missouri far to the east, and then later on, the giant Mississippi, that father of all waters, to empty through a great delta into the Gulf of Mexico.

This was the great divide—the roof of North America. If Solomon could imagine himself a giant spilling a mighty pail of water over these mountain peaks, the water would find its way down the sides of the mountain in just this way. By various routes they would find an ocean to refill.

Above this magnificent scene stretched a beautiful blue sky without a single cloud anywhere. The picture was sublime. It gives a man a feeling of great planning and at the same time of utter simplicity. How simple nature is! How well planned!

Somewhere in the Talmud Solomon had read that there had been two creations. A wise sage had said that the world had been created to be destroyed and then created again. "Did the Lord try to improve on His original work?" Solomon wondered.

He wished that he had a lens sensitive enough to photograph these same mountains at night. It looked like heaven itself when the moon had set and the night, dry and pure, seemed to have a light of its own, independent of the moon. In this pure frosty darkness, he could see what appeared to be millions of galaxies. Without any trouble he could find the star Orion, Aldebran, and the constellation called the Pleiades. It seemed as though the scene could not be real—as though it had been painted by a master hand. The silence gave one the feeling that there was no atmosphere.

He had gotten up early at the first sign of light to take pictures. Generations of Americans must know that their country was indeed very beautiful.

He stood in the snow buffing the plate with the long buffer until the plate looked no longer silver but black. He took care that the strokes should go in a direction parallel to the bottom of the finished daguerreotype. Thus, if there were any scratches to spoil the lines, they would not be seen as they would not be in the path of the light and would not cast any shadows. Every once in a while he would have to clean the buff with a buff-brush to remove the excess chemical. Finally, he picked up a second buff and passed the flannel, coated with a layer of jeweler's rouge, over the surface.

Buffing made for a clear picture. It distributed the silver all over the copper base so that the finished product would be perfect. Solomon wanted the print to be worthy of the beautiful scene.

Solomon next slipped the plate into the front part of the box. He trained the lens to get the view he wanted and removed the shutter in front so that the light would enter. He counted three and then removed the exposed plate, putting it into a plate holder which he closed with the little bone button that held it tight. This would protect the plate from any other light until he could wash away the unused chemical and reveal the picture.

Several times Solomon repeated the process until he had six or seven views of the peaks around him. Then, satisfied, he crossed to the camp to wash the plates in the clear water of the waterfall. The men, looking at the results, commented on the beauty of the copper plates. Truly, they were works of art. He packed the instruments away together with the pictures.

It was these pictures which were on his mind when they proceeded on their way the next morning.

Solomon followed in his usual place at the end of the line. Suddenly, the call, "Look out below!" made him look up.

What Solomon saw was frightening. The whole cavalcade of mules and horses was tumbling down the mountainside. From what Solomon could see, the first mule had lost its footing and before it could recover itself, had tumbled head over heels into the snow, dragging the other animals with it. One after another, they fell like pins in a bowling alley, thoroughly frightened. Fifty animals all braying from fear can make a lot of noise.

It was lucky that Solomon had stepped aside out of the trail in a hurry or he would have been caught in that snowslide. When the pitching and tossing was over, the men rushed to the place where the baggage and animals lay tangled in a hopeless mess. Everyone had to help with the goods, the buffalo hides, the cooking utensils and the scientific instruments. Solomon's thoughts immediately went to his photographic materials. He ran from one animal to the next, to see whether he could find his boxes. When he did find them, he saw that they had been able to stand up against the terrific fall. They were unharmed. Solomon was glad that he had had the foresight to build strong cases when he left St. Louis. His day's work in the village on the Kansas River had been worthwhile.

One of the horses and one of the mules had been killed and one of the horses had to be shot as it was in great pain.

To add to their discomfort, a new storm was blowing up and the Colonel ordered the men to make camp at the spot. The tent poles for the men's lodge had been broken in the fall and from now on, no matter what the weather would be, they would have to sleep in the open.

The despair of the men was so great that Colonel Fremont thought it wise to declare a halt so that they could rest from the difficult march. The men welcomed this.

But about midnight, when all were asleep, Solomon felt water trickling in between his clothes and his body. Since it was dark and the campfire had gone out, there was nothing that could be done but wait until morning.

With the dawn the men awoke and made a fire to dry out their clothes. Again Solomon rushed out to see if his daguerreotype material was safe before he took any steps to make himself comfortable. Luckily, his cases had been able to withstand the water.

Solomon was fond of saying that he was glad that his photographs and photographic instruments did not need food. Unfortunately, the men did. On that day, as on so many others, they went to bed without supper.

The march continued and for Solomon it was no longer a thrill to feel that they were on top of the world. The mountains were showing a new and terrible face. No longer did one think of their beauty. Only their cruelty could be felt now.

10 *New Year's Day, 1854*

The first day of January, 1854, found the men gradually ascending the slopes of the country between the Missouri River and the Rocky Mountains. Mr. Egloffstein and Carvalho awoke at the same time and together pushed up their covers, which had been made heavy by the fall of snow. As they did so they expected and got the usual shower of snow from their rubber blankets. It was one way of waking up, though not the most pleasant, and the men wiped the snow from their faces without impatience, as though this was the normal thing and to be expected.

The Swedish engineer looked up at Carvalho from his kneeling position as he rolled up the rubber blankets and fur robes.

"A good year to you, my friend. Have you made your New Year's wish? Now, don't answer," he said as his friend began to speak, "I know what you've wished for. It is your wife's chicken that she serves on Friday night. Well, I have put in my order first for Swedish smorgasbord with some glugg to wish you a happy New Year in my own favorite drink."

Solomon laughed. The engineer was always in a good humor and made a very fine companion. He loved to eat and was always talking about the superiority of Swedish cooking. Solomon of course, would uphold Jewish cooking as the best.

New Year or not, it was necessary for the group to move on. By this time the camp was awake and everyone was packing. Captain Wolff and his Delaware Indians were not aware of the change in the calendar. To them it was another day in the march.

But Mr. Fuller, assistant engineer to the expedition, was putting on his "best footwear" as he called it in fun. He was making a show of tying the rags around his feet as though they were his very best leather boots which he used for special occasions.

These jokes of the campfire were not really funny but they kept spirits up. So long as the men could laugh at their difficulties, there was hope that they would win through.

The Colonel appeared at his lodge entrance.

"Good morning, gentlemen," he said in his pleasant voice. There was no knowing whether he had slept or not. Those of the men who had been on watch that night knew that he had come out several times to make observations of the stars.

"May I wish you a good year?" and he shook hands all around. "You will be telling your families about this day and how you spent New Year of 1854."

Solomon spoke up.

"We may still have a better dinner than the families back home. I have saved a surprise for you."

"Is it the porcupine you would not eat?" said Captain Wolff. He could not resist teasing Carvalho about the experience of the previous week when Solomon had preferred to go hungry rather than eat the pink pork-like flesh of the porcupine they had shot.

"No," said Carvalho. "It will be as pink but much sweeter and certainly less fat."

Breakfast was eaten. Fortunately, the men on watch had been able to trap a rabbit. Fried over the fire, with biscuits of dough mixed with the juices from the meat, the rabbit gave the party something on which to start the day.

Tempers were good. Solomon Carvalho set the tone today. He remembered his experience of yesterday and shuddered. God had been good to him. Yesterday, once again, Solomon had been separated from the party. For a second time since he had joined the expedition he had been alone and had had to depend entirely on himself.

As usual, he had been at the rear of the cavalcade and had been following his pony, treading in its footsteps. The snow was deep and it was necessary many times to free himself from the drifts. As a result, his pony had gone ahead of him and the distance between himself and the rest of the party was at least fifty yards.

"Halloo," called Carvalho, but his voice was carried away by the wind.

It was in vain. Solomon was tired. He was undernourished and his strength was not sufficient to make himself heard.

However, the woodsman's instinct was strong within him and this prevailed over his feeling of despair. Solomon worked his way to the top of the mountain and from its height, looking on the other side, he saw the fresh tracks of horses. His breath was spent, but Solomon gathered his strength and in a last desperate effort, began to descend. Peering through the gathering dusk, he was able to make out a form moving, something gray. Was it another illusion? His weary eyes might be deceiving him. However, when he came down about ten or fifteen feet, he saw that it was his pony. It had been tied to a bush and there it stood with its back turned against the wind.

It was the work of a moment to mount it. Solomon forgot weariness and hunger. He rode the pony down to camp.

His comrades were waiting for him. They had

camp ready and their beds made. Food was ready, too, and another rabbit had been caught, this time by the Colonel, who had taken a quick shot from his seat in the saddle.

Solomon found out that it was Wolff who had tied up the pony, and thus certainly saved his life. In true Indian fashion, he gave Solomon no chance to thank him. But he did say, "Mr. Carvalho once gave me good medicine. He can thank the Great Spirit who saved me then. Captain Wolff knows not medicine but he knew when he saw Big Bill alone, that Solomon Carvalho had lost the party."

They had taken no break for the New Year as there was no reason why they should stop. However, the evening campfire found a very jolly company seated on their rubber blankets. The men had searched the hillside for wood and found enough for a fire. Solomon brought a very large kettle and with great pride emptied into it the Alden eggs and the pound of loaf sugar. He added the dried milk and the powdered sugar, and into this pudding-like mixture he placed the arrowroot which his wife had given him before leaving. The sweet smell of the arrowroot wafted in the air. In the meantime, the others were preparing the main part of the meal. The first course on the menu consisted of the usual horse soup, and then a dish of delicious horse steaks fried in the candle tallow which Carvalho had saved in his photograph cases.

The party ended with the pudding-à-la-Carvalho.

There were six gallons of the pink dessert, enough for everybody. No one complained because it had to be eaten in the tin plates of the campers instead of crystal glass.

"We have a magic man," said Captain Wolff. "He hide away things we no see. He make sweet magic."

Colonel Fremont took dinner with them that day. He called for a toast. Solomon would have liked to give them each a drink of the brandy that he had taken with him on this expedition. But there was none to spare so the Colonel toasted them all in some of the soup which was the only liquid they had.

"To a gallant company," he said. "To the men who have laid the way for the road which will cross the empire which is the future United States of America."

They certainly did not look like a gallant company that night huddled around the camp fire, nursing what warmth they could find. They were, of course, wearing all the clothes they had. There was no longer any thought of having baggage or knapsacks. They were a tattered, dirty company.

There had been no thought of washing clothes since the pleasant days of the Kansas River. Some of the company wore buffalo mittens which Solomon had sewn for them during those days. But the footwear, the moccasins he had made at the same time, had all been torn and one could glimpse, under the rags, the black feet which told the story of frostbite.

One could see, too, the sores which were scurvy. Scurvy was not only unsightly, it was also painful to the touch when one brushed up against a rock or even a tree.

But the Colonel was a leader in the true sense of the word. He could inspire his men to face death itself. Solomon thought back to the day in late August when he had entrusted his life to a man whom he had met for the first time. Solomon wondered again at the genius of this man who could make men forget despair and dare hope for success and triumph in the face of tremendous difficulties. Fremont evoked loyalty from his men. Never had they seen, nor would they ever see him expect less from himself than he did from his followers. Always in his mind was the certainty of success and this certainty he was able to communicate to his company.

Nothing could be heard in the stillness round the campfire but the hoot of an owl and the crackling of a burning limb of a tree as it fell into the fire from the smoldering trunk. Sparks flew from the fire in every direction, but the men, weary from their long day's march, did nothing to move away from them. The wind was obviously changing and the prediction was for colder weather. The Colonel rose to go.

"Good night, gentlemen, and thank you for a very pleasant evening."

The beds were made. The men lay as close as they could to the fire. The rubber mats kept them from the cold and wet of the ground and in teams of two, they lay down, watching the white clouds moving in a dark, star-studded sky. The granite peaks round them seemed to hem them in, in a circle tighter even than that of their guards.

Hardships of the Trail

11 *On Guard*

It was four o'clock in the morning when Solomon came off watch. He was not comfortable. In fact he was wet and cold. An upward movement in the air resulted in moisture being formed. Walking through foggy clouds was like walking through the spray coming from a large water hose. Being cold was uncomfortable enough but being wet and cold was worse. Moisture certainly was no insulation against cold.

But in spite of the wet and cold, Solomon was cheerful. He was proud of a job well done. To compete with the men of this expedition was a challenge. For the most part they were woodsmen who had lived on the edge of civilization for years or from birth and had learned early in life how to survive.

Though Solomon was a city-dweller, he had come through with honors.

To Solomon this was a tremendous satisfaction. Knowing that he had done his share of the camp guard duty and the camp chores with the rest was an accomplishment that he was proud of.

The artist in Solomon felt the beauty around him. The water rushing down the mountainside looked like a white-maned horse at full gallop. Its sound on the rocks below was like the booming of a cannon. Tomorrow this rushing water would no longer be beautiful. To cross this stream would take patience and determination. The horses would be unwilling to put their flanks into the current. When the riders would force the horses into the swirling waters, their bodies would hit the water with a dull thud and a great splash. Against their will, the horses would settle down to a long stride and would go forward in water which would often reach their chests and would be freezing cold. Progress would be slow and the rider would often find it hard to keep balance.

Suddenly Solomon felt a change in the weather. "Storm rising in the west," he said to himself. He shivered. He was getting soggier and soggier. The clouds surrounding him were so dense that they now hid the peaks around him. At five thousand feet they were almost invisible because of the clouds. A swirling storm was coming in.

He was just able to distinguish the form of things in the fog. He recognized the various trees by their shapes. There was the tamarack and the hemlock and the white bark pine. Here and there stood trees that had been burnt and blackened by lightning. Solomon remembered the first thunderstorms they had encountered. How the lightning whipped round the mountain peaks like a boy whipping a string round his top!

The trees around Solomon dwarfed him. He felt helpless at the thought of the forces of nature which could, if they wished, threaten a man with instant death. Lightning, glaciers, and avalanches stood ready to blot out the life of any man.

I wouldn't let my cat out on a night like this, he thought. This was the standing joke which Solomon always left to his relief guard and which he had said to Fuller as he turned to go back to bed. Fuller had smiled at the joke.

The sight of a carcass hanging near the fire reminded Solomon that he was hungry. He walked over and with his hunter's knife, cut himself a generous slice. It tasted sweet. Solomon remembered how he had shuddered just two months ago, when he had seen an Indian do this.

Well, a man grows. He learns not to be fussy about uncooked meat. And now, with something under his belt, a man could sleep. Four hours' sleep would be useful in getting ready and fit for tomorrow's march.

Around him lay the huge mounds that looked like living graves. Solomon stood near the mound which he shared with Egloffstein. Snow had covered it to make it look like an Eskimo igloo. It was the work of a moment to brush off the snow and to prepare to creep in beside his mate. He decided to smoke a pipe first.

At that moment he noticed a movement at the Colonel's lodge. The flap was raised and the Colonel's head appeared, followed by his lean body. The Colonel stopped to adjust his gloves in the frosty air. Mittens were bulky so the Colonel kept one pair of gloves to help him handle his instruments and log books.

The wind had changed and there was an increase in cold. The night became clear again as the wind swept away all the cloud banners. There was a decided change in weather and the Colonel, sensitive to all changes in weather, had come out of his tent to make observations. He noticed Carvalho and nodded to him, correct in his behavior even at this hour in the morning.

Solomon thought this a good opportunity to enjoy a quiet talk with this unusual man. Knocking out his pipe, he approached the Colonel.

"Good morning, sir," he said.

"Good morning, Mr. Carvalho. Have you noticed a change in the wind?"

"Yes, sir," returned Solomon. "It has been unsteady since about three o'clock."

"This has been the pattern of the weather for several days now," said the Colonel. "Our synoptic charts show that this is usual. The weather is due to change one way or another."

Half talking to himself, the Colonel continued, "Modern science has done wonderful things to help us in understanding the weather. And to think that it was one of our own American patriots who started us on the right path in this study."

"Who was that?" inquired Solomon, ever ready to learn something from this man.

"It was Benjamin Franklin," returned the Colonel. "He observed that weather moved from one place to another, carrying with it the same sort of atmosphere. He had noticed, for instance, that a storm in Philadelphia moved to Boston. This was in 1743. Studies confirmed this and scientists were well on the way to a new science—the science of Meteorology."

The Colonel handed Solomon his Forten barometer and, as he had been taught, Solomon removed the leather bag and adjusted the screw at its lower end. The mercury in the barometer rose. From the measurement Carvalho was able to see that they had gone a thousand feet higher than their position on the day before. He reported this fact to the Colonel.

"Very good, Mr. Carvalho," he said. "However, we will have to take into consideration the change in weather so the reading will probably be slightly different. I will look at the tables when I go into my tent later on."

"Let us check the clinometer," said the Colonel and he took from his pocket a very small instrument which helped him measure the slopes of the valley and compare it with the vertical sides.

"Now, let us move to another spot," said the Colonel.

Carvalho followed in his footprints. To his mind came the expression he had once heard about the Colonel. Someone had called him a "human bubble of vanity." Carvalho didn't agree with this criticism. If everyone were lucky enough to take a trip with Fremont, he would understand the greatness of this man.

Their next measurement had to be taken from another angle. To reach this spot, they were forced to go into a field of snow which reached to their waists. Round them the only sounds heard were the swirling snow and the coughing of the horses as they munched the grass in one of the meadows in the sheltered valley.

The Colonel continued to check the various angles. Carvalho watched the Colorado River. The many snowy peaks about them gave rise to the numerous brooks which, joined together, would in time form a giant one. The Colonel went on with his mathematical calculations. Carvalho saw in his imagination a vision of hundreds of scientists one day entering this region to take weather observations and sending out the information by the new method of communication called the telegraph. The electric telegraph would accelerate the understanding of this branch of science. The work of the Smithsonian Institute would grow and men would understand at last the behavior of the atmosphere.

Again, as in so many things in the past, the Colonel would be the leader. People would think twice before calling him names.

Solomon was interrupted in his meditation by the voice of the Colonel.

"Let us go back," he said.

At the open circle, the Colonel bade him farewell, still in his formal manner.

"Good morning," he said. "Good morning, Mr. Carvalho. Thank you for your help."

"Good morning and thank you, sir," said Solomon.

Suddenly he remembered that he had not asked the Colonel for permission to come.

12 *The Oath*

The company had now reached the Green River, a branch of the mighty Colorado River, and were deep in the snows of Utah. If conditions had been bad before, they were easy compared with what lay ahead. There were days when the men camped without the necessary wood to make a fire. They often had to lie down in their beds under their blankets in order to keep warm.

Food consisted of soup made of the intestines of the animals they killed. Since there was no water to be had, the entrails were shaken out in the snow and boiled in water made of melted snow. No part of the animal was left uneaten. The hide was roasted and the hair burnt off and this crisp skin was eaten, too. Since food was scarce, the hooves and shins had to be eaten and each man took a turn in receiving these undesirable portions.

The blood of the animals slaughtered was saved in a huge kettle and drunk by the men. As the animals were killed, an Indian would hold a dish under the slashed throat to receive the blood.

Solomon Carvalho could never bring himself to drink this blood, though he knew that it would give him strength to continue on the trail. He recalled the law of Moses which forbade Jews to use the blood of animals and so held out at the sickening sight.

Division of the food was a problem. When men are hungry, they become like children, ready to quarrel for a mouthful of food. To prevent quarrels, a system of division was set up. Each animal slaughtered had to last six days, unless another animal died which would give them additional unexpected food. The animal was divided into twenty-two portions. Two of these were put aside for the Colonel and his cook, Lee. Ten portions were given to the Indians and ten to the white men of the party.

The white men could never seem to deny themselves their food. They often took from the pile of meat when no one was looking. Thus they would really be robbing themselves. Thus, too, it would happen that the white men would be out of food when the Indians would still have some. Both the Colonel and the Indians seemed always to have some food put by while the white men were always hungry.

Division of food among the white men became a very important procedure. To prevent quarreling, they invented a system which would have been laughable if it were not so tragic. It looked like the kind of game that children would play.

The cook would stand with a piece of meat in his hand which he held behind his back. Each person would then choose one of these pieces. If his piece happened to be a little smaller than his friend's, he could not complain against anyone. He could grumble about "luck," though this did not help his aching stomach.

The camp lived on horsemeat for fifty days during this time and the white men would find themselves without food for as much as two or three days at a time.

It was a job keeping the mules alive by getting them to drink water, since there was so little food for them. Some of the mules would eat the snow around them, but for others it was necessary to melt the snow before they would touch it.

For the forty miles between the Grand and Green rivers, the land was barren and there was no water to be had. Solomon, while crossing this stretch, was so thirsty that he did what the animals might have done. He put his tongue under an artemisia bush and lapped up a bit of loose snow lying there. This was part of the job of keeping alive.

Keeping alive was a job that they had to work at all day. Scouting for wood in this barren country involved all the men and sometimes even the Colonel would take a hand at finding bits of twigs and fallen trees to warm them and to cook what food they did have.

The Colonel usually ate his meals alone in his lodge as he did not like to see his men suffering so. It was somewhat of a surprise to the men when they saw the Colonel come out and seat himself with the men around the fire. The wood had burned down and there was little light so that it was almost impossible for the men to see one another.

The Colonel spoke up.

"There is a matter of great importance that I would like to bring to your attention."

No one spoke and the darkness settled more firmly round them. Far off, the howl of a coyote and the bray of a frightened mule could be heard.

The Colonel continued.

"We are going through difficult times. This we will have to stand up to as best we can. I am firmly convinced that we will win. Remember, you are not the first to have made your way up through these mountains. The West was opened by men like Kit Carson and it is being opened in our day by others. There are sacrifices to be made, just as you are making sacrifices today."

What the Colonel was leading up to, nobody could guess.

"There have been a number of immigrant parties that have found their way over the Rockies to the lands in the Far West. Of these parties you may have heard of one called the Donner party."

It was coming out and now the men had a better idea of what their leader was trying to say.

The Colonel continued.

"In the course of crossing the Sierras during '46, the party found itself in a position similar to ours. Of course they were burdened with women and children which made their going more difficult. We do not have little ones to worry about."

There was not a sound as the Colonel went on.

"But these are the facts: We have a long way to go and much to face before we reach the Pacific. We will have to discipline ourselves to this way of living for as much time as need be. I cannot say to you that it will take two weeks or even two months. All I can say to you is that we will win through."

The Colonel knew how to make men face the facts, thought Solomon, huddled in his blankets.

"I know that we'll win through. We have not lost one life. We are still the same number as when we left Brent's Fort. But if we do face death, let us face it like men. In one particular I am especially determined that we act as men."

The Colonel's voice was firm and there was no question that he would be obeyed.

He continued: "The Donner party betrayed one law of society—the one law that distinguishes man from animal. They ate the meat of the bodies of those who died. This is what I have come to ask you. I

am asking each of you to swear before God and your friends that no matter what happens, we will not stoop to deeds which are not worthy of men. We will not stoop to deeds which are not human."

One by one, the Colonel called the name of each man there by the dead fire, and all swore that they would obey the promise they made there, not to eat human flesh.

"Before we go, there is one more thing," said the Colonel. "If any one breaks the solemn vow made here in the sight of your comrades and your God, I will shoot that man."

It was a scene that would be remembered by everyone there until his dying day. The men went to bed without speaking.

13 *Lost in the Snows*

"We are lost, lost!"

Mr. Fuller was sitting in the snow huddled like a child who has been punished. His face was hidden in his hands and his body shook with sobs. It was pitiful to see a grown man give way to despair. The broad-shouldered, hardy engineer who had joined the party in September had been the picture of energy and enthusiasm. Looking at him now, Solomon saw only a shell of a man.

What can one do for a friend at a time like this, Solomon wondered. For Mr. Fuller's sake he was grateful that the rest of the party was plodding on in the distance and could not hear the sobs of the engineer. There was little left of the interesting companion that he had enjoyed so much on the trail.

Carvalho tried to think of words of encouragement that he could use to help his friend. He fell back on the words which the Colonel himself had used only yesterday.

"Buck up, man. This is the time that tests men and I know that you can make it. It's times like these when a man lives at his height. Just when he thinks he's beaten he gets his second wind. Then he can push forward to greater glory."

Fuller stopped crying. He tried to get up. With the help of Solomon and Egloffstein, Fuller was able to stand. Fortunately the day was drawing to a close and they would soon rest. Solomon saw with a photographer's eye how the winter sun set over the mountains in front of them. How he wished that he could record this for the people at home! But how would he find the strength to lift down the large packing cases that kept the camera and instruments safe on the baggage mules' backs?

They trudged ahead in the huge footsteps of the men ahead of them, and found themselves in deep drifts which reached to their necks.

Solomon wondered at fate. Mr. Fuller had been the strongest and largest in camp when they left Westport. Of all men, he seemed to be the best suited to bear the hardships of the trail. Yet as events had turned out, he had been the first to break down.

As though completing Carvalho's thoughts, Mr. Fuller suddenly collapsed. They supported him more firmly and found that even with help, Mr. Fuller would be unable to drag one foot after an-

other—he had become paralyzed. His friends sat
him down on what seemed to be a rock and prepared
to stay with him. Mr. Fuller had a better understanding of the situation than they had. He refused
to allow them to stay.

"Go," he said, "and if you can send me help from
camp, do so. You can do no good for me by remaining here. And if you do not reach camp before night-
fall, we shall all freeze to death."

Fortunately the poor man had his blue blankets
strapped to his back and his two friends wrapped
them round him. They looked round them for an
old bush or something to make a fire—but there was
nothing but one vast wilderness of snow around
them. So they made him as comfortable as they could
and left him.

"Take care not to fall asleep," Mr. Egloffstein
called. "We will have help come to you before you
know it."

"Remember not to leave the trail," was Solomon's
warning. He was thinking of every precaution
though he knew that the sick man could hardly
move his body.

The photographer and Mr. Egloffstein moved off
with as much speed as they could. They were determined to save their comrade. They realized that
night was falling fast and that the temperature was
falling, too. It was necessary to get their bearings so
they climbed to the top of a high hill and looked for
their party. But nothing could be seen and they had

to be content to follow the tracks and thus hope to come up to the rest in time. The trail seemed endless. After ten hours they came to camp.

The two went together to tell the Colonel about Mr. Fuller. Fremont's face looked sad as he said, "I'm sorry, gentlemen. But I cannot allow one more person to jeopardize his life in this case."

It seemed so cruel a decision that Carvalho fell to the ground crying. He did see the wisdom of the judgment. There was no way out of it. Only a few animals were left and they were needed to carry the baggage and the scientific apparatus. Then, too, with the storm, it would not be an easy task to find the trail which by now would be covered up with the new snow drifts.

Carvalho had seen the look of anguish which had covered the face of the Colonel while he was giving his decision. In his mind, his remaining power of reason said, "When the lives of so many men are in danger, it would not be right for one man to expect the group to sacrifice their lives for him."

But his heart was saying in the tradition of the Talmud, "This is a human being, created in the image of God. How can we leave him? Does the Talmud not say, 'He who saveth a life is as though he saveth a city?' "

Solomon was resigned when he left the Colonel's lodge. One had to think of the greater good. It was a cruel dilemma.

Outside, the group was discussing the unfortunate

decision when suddenly the flap of the Colonel's lodge was raised and the Colonel appeared. Turning to Moses and Welachus, two of the Delawares, he told them to take the best animals from the transport and to pack some horsemeat soup. He then asked Frank Dixon, a Mexican, to find Mr. Fuller. The Colonel hoped from the description of the location that the man was not more than five miles from the present campsite.

The hours that went by were more tense than any the men had ever experienced. It was hard to sit and wait and wonder what was happening a few miles away. No one slept and there was not a dry eye in the camp. The Colonel came out often to ask whether there was any news from the rescue team. At dawn there was still no sign of them. In spite of his usual reserve and silence, the Colonel was heard to say, "This is what I expected. I should never have sent anyone out."

As usual he blamed himself and no one else.

Carvalho was more affected than anyone else. It was at his request that the rescue had been attempted. He felt that he had sent a man to certain death.

At daylight, the Colonel sent three Delawares to find the missing men. After six hours of nervous waiting, the men were delighted to see one Delaware coming into camp with Frank Dixon.

Experienced though Frank was as a guide and

traveler, he had become bewildered in the snow-storm and had fallen down in the snow.

"Fortunately," he said later on in telling the story, "I had hold of the line that leads the donkey and so I was saved."

When they found him he still held the lead line in his frozen hand.

Later, the Delawares came into camp with Mr. Fuller. The poor man was trembling from the cold and was unable to recognize anyone. Solomon was overjoyed and ran to fetch the last drop of alcohol left in his instrument cases. To make it last longer, he mixed it with some of the water made from melted snow. Mr. Fuller thanked him with his eyes.

Solomon tried to stop thinking of the many problems which would be added to those they already had. Fuller's feet were frozen to the ankles and would have to be amputated as soon as possible. But more important for the present was the fact that Mr. Fuller would be an added burden to a situation already difficult to bear.

Had they done the right thing in endangering the lives of the group for this one man who from now on would be nothing but a handicap? And suppose someone else became ill? Could they stop and nurse such a person or should they go on and leave him? Suppose that person was Solomon himself—would that change his opinion and could he have the courage to tell his comrades to go on without him?

Solomon knew that a situation of that sort might well arise. On one previous morning he had wakened to a feeling of dullness and inertia. He felt unwilling to get out of bed. He was unequal to facing the sorrows of the day and was prepared to let the others go on alone. Fortunately, his natural will to live revived and he got out of bed.

There was magic in life after all. He enjoyed the natural beauty around him as he returned to the hardships of the trail.

14 *Licked!*

The Sierras had him licked!

Solomon Carvalho sat in the snow, his feet resting in the footprints of those who had gone on before him. The party filed on, all on foot, following the baggage which had been packed on the last remaining mules, now reduced to twenty-two animals.

Solomon no longer thought of survival and ultimate victory. He felt that his last hour had come. It took courage and will to push oneself forward on the long trail and Solomon had lost that desire. From the top of the mountain he peered from between eyelids swollen by the wind and the glare of the sun on the bright snow. The whiteness of the snow hurt his eyes. Not even a tree was there to relieve the constant glare. His feet were cold and weary. He was too cold to feel, too blinded to see, and too weak to move. He was licked.

Solomon began to weep with self-pity, like a child whimpering when he is ill. He hadn't the strength to pull one frozen foot after the other and he had hardly the strength to cry. His awful loneliness made him think of his family. Solomon wanted to say goodbye to his wife and children and then find eternal peace. With difficulty he removed the buffalo mitten on his right hand and blew on his stiffened fingers to warm them. With difficulty he reached into the pocket of his jacket.

Through heavy eyelids he peered at his smiling family in the photograph before him. He remembered the warmth of the Friday evenings in his home, before there had been any thought of trips into the Far West. He recalled the candles shining on the table and they seemed to bring him warmth. He saw the Sabbath bread lying on the white Sabbath tablecloth. It seemed to him that the cloth lay all around him as far as the eye could reach in the Utah trail. It was just about sundown and he pictured his wife, smiling and lighting the tapers.

Solomon smiled, too, like a child. Just so did Charity, his daughter, smile while looking into the lights. Solomon was unwilling to leave the scene. He was unwilling to part from his family and the beautiful tradition of the Jewish home. He was quite prepared to lay down his head and enjoy the peace of the evening.

Had he done so, he would have suffered the fate of so many wanderers who, in a weakened physical

condition, robbed of the fighting instinct, rested for
a moment in the snow. If anyone stopped in the trail
and sat down, even for an instant, there was the
danger that he could not then find the energy or will
to get up and so would remain in the snow to fall
into a deep sleep from which there would be no waking. This was the dread of all travelers in the
snow.

Carvalho was aware of this situation from books
he had read and from the constant warnings of the
Delaware Indians around the campfire. Previously, he
had never felt this urge but the illness of his good
friend, Fuller, and his own weakened condition were
sapping his strength. Today his poor tired brain refused to serve his thin body. Solomon felt that his
last hour had come.

Ahead of him, the party had just disappeared behind the white curve of a mountain. The whole
thing looked unreal to him like something from another world. The slow movement of the line of men
and animals and the eerie silence was like a dream.
No one had the energy or desire to sing or shout or
even talk. The animals, too, were dumb in every
sense of the word, responding wearily to the kick of
the mule-driver or the prodding of a stick.

Around him lay a desert—not the torrid desert of
the Africas, but a desert nevertheless—with nothing
growing on it for miles around. Even God had de-
serted them, thought Solomon.

"*Le-cha, dodee, Lik-rat kala*, Come my beloved

and meet the bride," sang Solomon through his cracked lips. He was welcoming the Sabbath in the lovely melody of the Sefardi Jew.

The word "come" lingered in his brain. It seemed to be reminding him of something important. The bright little voice of his daughter seemed to be calling for a drink from her bedroom beyond the dining room. Her father rose as though to fulfill her request. A need was there and he, as faithful father and provider, must not fail his family.

His family needed him. He had to break through, no matter how great the difficulties might be. He had something to live for. He could not forsake them. They looked to him for support. He just couldn't sit there forever. Solomon was brought back to reality. Sleep could be fatal and daydreams were the beginning of sleep. He rose and voiced his thanks to God who had helped him in his time of great need.

In the course of the trip he had become a woodsman in the best Fremont tradition. He took out his gun and his pistol and carefully examined them. Gone was the tenderfoot who had left his gun behind him in those early days on the Arkansas River. Solomon had learned his lessons well. He was ready and so were his guns.

Nature didn't seem cruel any more, though he knew that there might be enemies lying in wait for him. It was getting dark and wolves might attack a lone man on the trail. This was the cycle of nature.

The stronger attack the weak and it was the duty of a man to see that he did not become weak. Eternal vigilance was the price of life.

It was well for Solomon that he had gotten his second wind. Night was coming on and a fearful storm blew directly into his face. He had to brace himself against its fury. So he bent down, and plodded along. He walked through the storm and when it abated, he was still walking. The sky was now studded with stars and the cold frosty air made a ghostly picture round him. Yet he felt at ease as he savored the beauty of the scene. But not for a moment did he let go of the pistol.

For the last hour before ten o'clock it became almost pleasurable as he walked in the footprints of his friends, toward refuge. His friends saw him coming and hallooed to him. There was none of the buffoonery of the last time or the teasing about him being late. But the Colonel was sitting near the fire and Solomon knew that he had been waiting for him. Solomon's coming had a special meaning for his leader. It showed that man could and would always be able to pit himself against the obstacles which nature raises and win through.

"Ah, there you are, Mr. Carvalho. I knew that you would be coming in soon."

Solomon remembered the words and the tone of the voice throughout his life. The Colonel's voice was steady and calm, as though this was all in a day's work.

Solomon smiled, a smile that was somewhat hidden behind the whiskers and dirt around his mouth.

Suddenly Solomon Carvalho felt himself going backward. He was about to fall. Instinctively he threw back his foot and saved himself from falling into the snow. The brain cannot think when the stomach is so empty and Solomon's reflexes were slow. But in his fuddled senses he realized that it was the Colonel's fault. The man he trusted had given him a slight push on the chest which had been enough to topple him as he stood warming his poor bones beside the campfire. Again tears welled up in Carvalho's eyes—this time tears of anger.

Then the calm voice of the Colonel came through the mist which surrounded him. The Colonel seemed to be talking to himself out loud and in a pleased way, as though he had been arguing with himself and had proved something to himself.

"He hasn't given up. Thoroughbreds never do."

Then looking at Carvalho he said, "You are good for a good many miles yet, Solomon Carvalho. There is still will and purpose in you and strength to stand up against any of the vicissitudes facing us."

Except for a few Delawares who happened to be nearby at the time, the others had been unaware of what had happened. No one had heard the words spoken except Solomon himself. But the incident left Solomon with a feeling that life was not as serious or as impossible as it had seemed up to this point.

Later on, after their poor supper of horsemeat

soup, the Colonel called Solomon into the lodge and explained his action, apologizing for doing it in such an unexpected manner. Seated in the lodge with his superior, Carvalho listened to the words of a man who had faced death many times.

"There is only one thing that will keep you alive and that is the will to live. When one loses the will, everything is over."

By showing that his reflexes were still functioning, Solomon had proven that all would still be well and the expedition would succeed. Solomon came out of the lodge with the words of his hero ringing in his ears: "When a man is beaten and pushes himself forward—that is when he lives. He is made strong by nature and he can face any odds. Only the weak die on the trail. Only those who succumb to a stronger force do not reach the goal."

Solomon crept into his blankets and huddled against Egloffstein for warmth. In his head the melody of the *Lecha Dodee* went round and round. But there were new words to the song: "The Sierras did not whip me. They will not whip me. I will be back with my family very soon."

15 *Put Not Your Trust in Princes*

"Put not your trust in princes."

Solomon remembered this saying from the Talmud. To him Fremont was indeed a "prince among men." Solomon looked at him standing on the very peak of the mountain in the Wasatch Range. Physically, he was still a prince—a commander, in control of every situation, no matter how dangerous. Nothing could make him bend, neither cold nor starvation nor want.

Now it seemed as though he had lost his senses.

Yesterday in his council meeting with Captain Wolff, Fremont had been unmoving in his decision.

"Captain Wolff," he had said, "we have one question before us. We cannot stop to think *if* we are to go to the top of this mountain before us. We have only to decide *how* best to do so."

Carvalho had heard every word of the talk. He was at the moment standing almost up to his middle in snow with the thermometer registering forty degrees below zero. This was the night that the star Cerus would be hidden by the moon and the Colonel especially wanted readings to be taken so that a very exact latitude and longitude would be available.

Solomon worked on, using the light of a sperm candle that he had set aside when they had buried their stores in the snow. After taking the angles of the star in question, he turned his mind and attention to another job which the Colonel had given him. He used his instruments to measure the height of the peak standing before him. He used his instruments very carefully so that the figures would be precise. One thousand feet of sheer rock stood in front of them. Solomon wondered how the Colonel hoped to climb one thousand feet of sheer precipice.

Burying the baggage seemed to be a decision which was the beginning of a new policy in the plans of the expedition. All the articles which were absolutely necessary were put aside. Everything else was put in large buffalo robes to be protected from the damp. Then the whole was lowered into a pit which had been dug in the snows. Surplus gunpowder, the daguerreotypes and the cameras, the scientific in-

struments which could be spared, and all the blankets that had been put away made a tremendous
pile. The company was traveling light from this day
forward.

"Now," said the Colonel, "we will climb this
mountain and three days will have us in Parowan.
You all have mounts. The mules are free from great
burdens since there is no baggage. But you must
walk part of the way. Our readings of latitude and
longitude are absolutely correct. There is nothing to
stand in our way. Let us go!"

On the following morning they did scale the
mountain. The travelers faced it with dread. It
seemed so steep that a human fly would not dare to
try it. But so great was the respect and admiration
that the men had for their leader that no one voiced
a fear or doubt.

There was no doubt on that day in February,
1854, that they would follow him downward, too.
The Colonel stood on the top of the high mountain
and held in his hand a pocket compass which he
looked at for some time. Then with his right hand,
in a dramatic gesture, he pointed in the direction
downward. Every movement was certain and clear.
There was no saying no to this man.

If going up the mountain had been hard, the
downward half was harder. None of them had shoes.
Some of them had rawhide tied round their feet,
while others were half covered with worn stockings

and moccasins. Even the Colonel's moccasins were tattered.

So they continued their journey. There was no hope that the men could ride their animals as the footing was poor. Frequently the animals would come slipping down the sides of the slopes and man and beast would brace themselves as best they could.

Winding down one mountain and crossing over to another, they kept on in the direction set out by their leader who was always in front. To add to their troubles, trees began to appear on the sides of the canyon and their going became rougher and rougher.

However, by noon of the next day, they found they had reached a narrow pass between two stiff cliffs. By following in single file, they were pleased and surprised to come to a little valley. Flowing through it was a lovely little creek and the men had their fill of cool, fresh water for the first time in weeks. The mules lost no time in beginning to eat the juicy grass which grew around them. It would have been impossible to tear them away from the fodder.

"Deer tracks," one of the Delaware stated. "Plenty deer!"

The thought of a juicy deer steak made the men's mouths water.

"My best gun to the man who brings us something from those tracks," said the Colonel.

The Indians were off without any delay while the

men rested on the grass. There had been no halt on the mountainside and the men were exhausted. Afterward, they gathered wood to make a fire on the sands. It was not long before Welachus was back, leading the rest of the Indians, and slung over the saddle of the leading mule was a beautiful buck Welachus had shot.

Each man toasted venison, Indian fashion, on willow sticks. Sore feet and tired bodies were forgotten as the men filled their stomachs. Though they could see no sign of a village, the men seemed a bit more optimistic about the Colonel's promise. This seemed to be a turning point in their luck.

The going was still rough and Fuller was uncomfortable. The poor engineer was struggling along and he was the only sign of despair in a situation which held a glimmer of hope. The man made no complaint and spoke no word. But the others could see that his strength was failing steadily.

He did not live to see their goal accomplished. Somewhere along the trail, his friends made a shallow grave with their hands and buried him, marking the spot with stones so that he could be buried properly at the first opportunity.

The Colonel was always in the lead. The pocket compass was never far from his hand. He seemed to be always consulting it and one could see that he seemed always to be making mental calculations which they would not have been able to understand

if he had told them. He had always seemed somewhat withdrawn and quiet but today he was utterly
silent. The men had no doubt that he was certain of
the way. They could only trudge over the difficult
terrain and trust.

Difficult days followed but the men were not as
despairing as they had been. Of course there was no
chance to rest or sleep because they had no covering,
so, except for the few halts that were called, it was
one continuous march through dull, never changing
scenery.

It was quite a cheerful party of men that reached
the village of Parowan. Yet their smiles were the
smiles of ghosts. Teeth and eyes seemed to make up the
whole face. The villagers wondered at this band of
men, tattered and torn, scarcely able to stand on
their feet from exhaustion and starvation.

The march was a triumph of man's ability to take
punishment yet defy death. It was a battle of will
against defeat. The people of Parowan wondered at
the miracle which had taken place.

It was indeed a miracle brought about by a man
who used knowledge and science to serve his ends.
The Colonel had saved them. Had he made a mistake of even a few miles, they would have missed the
little village nestled in the mountains. They might
have passed by the little hollow and gone on to
death.

Solomon was correct in his evaluation of the

Colonel. He had said, "My estimation of character is seldom wrong. I knew that day in September that I was safe with this man. At each crisis I have felt safer and safer, knowing that our lives were in the hands of a genius."

16 *Parowan*

The kind Heap family took care of Solomon as though he were a little child. Solomon remembered afterward in shame that he had cried like a baby when the three Heap children came into the room. Yet his tears were tears of joy. He had been saved for his own family.

Solomon was attended by two "Mrs. Heap." He could not understand this, since both seemed to be about the same age. Both of them referred to Mr. Heap as "my husband," and in his weakened physical condition Solomon was unable to comprehend. It was only afterward that he remembered. Of course! The Mormon religion allowed and even encouraged more than one wife for each husband.

The Heap family would have taken care of Solomon in any event, but the Colonel made it clear to the family that he wanted to defray the expenses of Mr. Carvalho's stay at their home. True to his word, the Colonel paid the Heap family the sum of one dollar and fifty cents per day for fourteen days. This pleased Mr. Heap very much as he was a man who knew the value of a penny and appreciated money. It was common gossip in the Mormon community that Mr. Heap was somewhat stingy and that his wives suffered from this weakness in his character. However, he was forgiven by those who could understand, since his childhood in London had been one of extreme poverty. From these poor people in England, Brigham Young, leader of the Mormons, had found his best recruits when he made plans to settle in the desert region of Salt Lake.

On the last day the Colonel came to visit Solomon and paid for his care. Solomon had taken on twenty pounds over the hundred and one which he had weighed on that first day in Parowan. He seemed to be restored in health and wished to go on with the Colonel. But the doctor refused to allow him to continue with the expedition, saying that Solomon's health had been affected by the poor food and that he needed time to improve.

Egloffstein, too, had to remain behind and it was decided that the two should go on to Salt Lake City to recuperate. Both men insisted that they felt quite well, but when it came time to mount their horses, they had to be lifted into the saddles.

When they were ready to go off, a surprise awaited

them. The Colonel came to see them off and wish them Godspeed.

"Would you like me to post any letters for you?" the Colonel asked. Solomon was grateful. It was a kind and thoughtful thing to remember. Little did either of them realize that these letters, together with the ones that Solomon had sent home to his wife at every opportunity, would be the material for a book that would be the only one written about the fifth trip of the Colonel. Nor could they know that this book would be printed again one hundred years afterward and would be read again and again by Americans who wanted a true story of the opening of the West. The name of Carvalho would live in the letters written to his wife in a book bearing the long title, "Incidents of Travel and Adventure in the Far West with Colonel Fremont's Last Expedition Across the Rocky Mountains, Including Three Months' Residence in Utah and a Perilous Trip Across the Great American Desert to the Pacific by S. N. Carvalho."

"Well, good-bye Mr. Carvalho and thank you for everything," the Colonel said in parting. "We will bring out your plates and have them developed for the report of our trip."

Then, turning to Egloffstein, "I shall look forward to seeing you gentlemen in Washington, where it will be my pleasure and that of Mrs. Fremont to welcome you in our home and thank you more formally."

He stepped aside to let the party move off and stood saluting them as they left. Solomon, turning round on his horse saw that the Colonel, with his usual courtesy and consideration, had remained for a final wave.

Solomon knew that it would be a long time before he would see this great man again. From now on, he was on his own, to pick up his life from where it had been changed by his meeting with the Great Pathmaker.

Solomon felt a little sad.

17 *Salt Lake City*

Solomon was back to his old profession but in entirely different surroundings. A room at Blair's Hotel in Salt Lake City was his studio and here he received many of the important men of the Mormon faith. Trade was good and Solomon could not complain about business. The sleepy little town was glad to find something interesting to change the dullness of the old routine. For those who could afford it, a visit to the daguerreotyper, now turned artist, was a nice way to brighten the monotonous pattern of the day.

It seemed only yesterday that Solomon had done this same preparation in his studio in Baltimore on the other side of the continent. He was preparing the oils for a portrait he had been commissioned to do. So much had happened since September 1853, that it seemed like a dream.

The human body is certainly a wonderful instrument, thought Solomon to himself. God gave us bodies that can take a great measure of punishment and then can snap back to their first state. I feel well and there seem to be no ill effects after our strenuous journey.

Solomon still remembered with a sort of shame his behavior when he came into Parowan in the Little Salt Valley—how his spirit suddenly gave way. The last three days of the journey were the worst physically and it was from utter weakness that he had sunk to the ground completely exhausted. He remembered how kind hands had picked him up and carried him to the house of Mr. Heap, preacher and shoemaker.

He remembered with disgust the picture of himself in the mirror of the Heap home. There he sat in the clean bed of the Mormon home, his hair long and his face unshaven. The dirt had been rubbed in as there had been no water with which to wash and no towel to dry his face on the rare occasions when there was water. His fingers were frostbitten and split at every joint. He was suffering from diarrhea and could not control himself. The scurvy had become worse and he was covered with sores and bruises from head to toe.

The journey to the Mormon capital had lain through the Great Basin which Fremont had surveyed and mapped so well on his previous trip. Egloffstein was determined that he would do something constructive, too, to help future travelers, and so he did some work with his instruments and spent some time making notes of the rocks and soil of the territory through which they were passing.

Solomon, struck with the desolate beauty of this territory, had none of his photographic material to work with, and could only make little sketches of the ten days' trip to the Mormon city.

So both men were kept busy, each one carrying on in the Fremont tradition of mapping the West.

The prayers of the synagogue came frequently to the mind and lips of the Jewish pioneer and he found himself humming some of the prayers of the Prayer Book. He found that one of the morning prayers seemed to suit his situation best, and he sang, "Blessed art Thou, Lord of the Universe, Who revivest the dead."

In Salt Lake City, it was hard to believe that he had gone to bed haunted by dreams of tables laden with all sorts of delicacies. These dreams of a hungry man had been like a mirage in the mind of a desert traveler who imagines that an oasis is within reach of his hands.

Solomon looked at the plate of apples which Sharon, the innkeeper's daughter had brought to him.

"You see," she said, "we have made the desert bloom like the rose."

"You have done better than that," returned Solomon. "You have made the desert bloom as the apple."

Solomon repeated these words afterward to the man who came for a sitting. It was none other than the Governor, Brigham Young. The Governor was pleased and he described to Solomon how they had brought water to the salt desert. It had taken a great deal of courage for the Mormons even to think of farming the poor soil and then to divert the water to irrigate the fields.

Solomon was curious about the name "Deseret" —the name the Mormons had given to this region.

"It means 'honey bee' in our Book of Mormons," said the Governor, "and it stands for industry and hard work."

"Truly," said Solomon as he painted away at the canvas in front of him, "you have indeed changed the desert to a land of milk and honey."

Solomon came to realize that Brigham Young was a man of destiny. He had a commanding appearance —almost like a soldier's. His had been the driving force behind the Mormon achievement. Even when he was relaxed, one could feel the strength of the man. Solomon put into this portrait the lines of determination and purpose that he saw in the face of the Mormon leader.

Governor Young was dressed for the portrait. He wore a proper afternoon frock coat, carefully tailored, and he was smartly combed and shaved. He was as well turned out as any diplomat about to step into a waiting carriage in Washington or Paris.

In fact, though this man was called an apostle, his outward appearance was more like that of a statesman of President Millard Fillmore's cabinet. He de-

served the title of statesman, because he had carved
out an empire or at least a great territory in what
had been wasteland.

It was said that Governor Young had seventeen
wives. To Solomon having more than one wife seemed
wrong. Yet this man seemed so honest and religious
that Solomon could not imagine Brigham Young guilty
of doing wrong. He steered clear from becoming en-
tangled in argument with the Governor, as he knew
that his religion encouraged him to have many
wives. Thus he was carrying out a precept of his religion and not breaking any law.

As for himself, he remembered the line in the
Book of Genesis which said "Therefore shall man
cleave unto his wife." Solomon felt sure that the sin-
gular person was used to emphasize that each man
was to have but one wife.

The Governor was speaking.

"You and I have something in common, Mr. Carvalho."

"What is that?" asked Solomon.

"We Latter Day Saints used Fremont's map to
find our way to Deseret."

Solomon was surprised. "I was not aware of that,
sir," he said. "The more I hear about this man, the
more I realize what a wonderful man he is and how
vast are his capabilities."

"Yes, that is true," said Governor Young. "Would
you be surprised to hear that the Colonel was the
first to sail on Salt Lake? In fact, he was the first

white man to sight the lake on September 1843, more than ten years ago. If it had not been for him, the Church of the Latter Day Saints would never have found this spot."

Solomon had yet three days in which to practice his art before he was to bid farewell to the territory of Utah and the kind Mormons who had befriended him. He was proud to be associated with these hardy pioneers who were making history. Before he left he was invited to be a guest at a party which was being held in the Governor's mansion.

Solomon was amused to see how the Governor was able to please all his wives. Surely no man could keep peace in a household with more than one woman, yet the Governor managed to make all happy.

The tables were loaded with good things of all kinds, as each lady brought food from her household. There were cakes and pies of many kinds and each item was artistically set out. No one seemed to have a care in the world. Solomon noticed that, in keeping with Mormon laws, there were no liquors served nor did anyone smoke.

The whole party showed dignity and merriment. This mood brought him memories of his own home and the social events he and his wife shared with their good friends. This was a little closer to the kind of civilization he was accustomed to. With God's help, he too would be home with his family.

18 *War or Peace?*

Egloffstein and Carvalho rode together down the trail southward from Salt Lake City. They had joined a party of missionaries who were on the way to the Sandwich Islands to convert the natives there to the Mormon faith. Egloffstein was to leave them at one of the Mormon villages on his way to join Captain Gunnison's party now under the leadership of Lieutenant Beale.

Mr. Egloffstein was laughing and his great body shook.

"Our mules had a much easier time when we rode up just two weeks ago," he said.

"Sixty pounds for me," said Solomon. "It seemed as though I could never stop eating. Everything seemed so good—the Mormon butter and the fresh eggs and the pastries. Even though brown sugar was a dollar a pound, I couldn't seem to deny myself anything. As a result I am twenty pounds heavier than I ever weighed in Baltimore."

"That is what happened to me," said Egloffstein and he laughed again. "I was invited to the Governor's ball as you know, but I was unable to find a ready-made suit to fit me so I had to stay home. Perhaps when I have been on this trip with Lieutenant Beale I will lose some of this surplus fat. We are to continue the work of Gunnison and explore a pass in the Sierra Nevada Mountains. Among other objectives I must begin to think of earning some money. I have none."

He became serious. Solomon remained silent. He did not want to boast, but he had done very well in Salt Lake City. He had earned a great deal of money with his paintings and had been able to outfit himself with everything he needed including clothes of the very best quality and things to make himself comfortable for the trip. With this, Solomon had been able to provide himself with plenty of food for the trip—crackers and sardines and sugar and coffee. He also had a pocket compass, a thermometer and even drawing material.

Though well into the month of May, it was still chilly, and after Solomon had covered three miles, a severe storm set in. On the next morning it was still snowing heavily, but Solomon decided that he would continue as he was anxious to join Governor Young, who was waiting for him at Petetnit.

It was remarkable to see what the Mormons had done to improve the land. Solomon passed town after town which had been erected in this previously barren land. At each village there were almost a thousand people and every settlement had large herds of cattle and horses and a saw mill and a flour mill.

At one of these towns called Pleasant Grove, Solomon stopped to warm his frozen bones and eat a meal. Then he continued on his way, snow blowing in his face for the full distance of almost twenty miles.

In Petetnit the Governor met him. A crowd of people came out to see their chief and to receive his blessing. As their religious leader, he performed this rite. Solomon could not help but smile. He might as well be back in his own synagogue. The Governor's blessing sounded just like the one a rabbi would give to his congregation.

The Governor was on an important mission for his people, one that would bring either peace or trouble to his settlements. The Indian tribes were on the warpath. They were headed by an Indian chief called Wakara, often called Walker instead. Captain Gunnison and an engineering party on the way west had been attacked and the captain and many of his men murdered by the Indians. The

white men were afraid that this might be the beginning of a terrible Indian war that would affect the
Mormon villages. Governor Young had chosen to go
to the great chief Wakara to speak to him.

There didn't seem to be too much hope for peace.
When they approached the camp of Wakara, he sent
word that if the Governor wished to see him, he
could come to him. Wakara did not intend to travel.

This Young decided to do, so determined was he
to bring peace to the Utah Valley. Though he was a
governor, Wakara was a king in his own right and
had all the privileges of a king.

The white men found that Wakara treated them
with courtesy. He had an honor guard meet them
and escort them into the village to his lodge.

Wakara sat on a buffalo robe wrapped in blankets.
He did not rise to greet them but offered his hand to
Young and made room for him at his side. They all
shook hands.

In the circle with the Chief and the white men sat
the Indian chiefs of the tribes—the Pahutes, the
Pravins and Payedes. Among other Indian celebri-
ties were Ammon, Squash Head, Grosepine and
Kanoshe. The interpreter was a Mr. Huntington.
He made known to them why the Governor had
come and hoped that they could smoke a calumet of
peace and that there would be no cause for hard
feeling.

The Chief sat silently, as did everyone else.

Finally after five minutes' silence, one of the chiefs rose. His name was San Pete. As he rose, his robes slipped from him and they could see a body bearing many scars. He spoke in English.

"I am for war. Americats kill Indian plenty. One year gone. Mormon say they no kill Indian. Mormons no tell truth. Plenty Ute Indians go to Great Spirit. Mormon killed them."

Then he went on: "My son—brave and good child. Good to his father and old mother. One day Wa-yo-sha hunt rabbits and food for old people. Rifle of white man kill him. Mother go see. Find son killed. White men shoot bullet. Kill wife. Now San Pete no can fight more. Old San Pete dim eyes and hands tremble. Murderers of wife and brave Wa-yo-sha still living. San Pete no make peace with Americats."

Young asked Wakara to speak.

All Wakara would say was, "No got heart speak— no can talk today. Tonight Wakara talk with Great Spirit. Tomorrow Wakara talk with Governor."

Governor Young knew that he must wait. He handed the pipe to Wakara who took it and gave one or two whiffs and then the Governor smoked it. It was then passed round among the men that sat at the fire and everyone puffed it once or twice.

While all this was going on, Solomon sat with his pencil and paper, sketching the head of Kanoshe, the chief of the Pravin tribe, whom he found a fascinating study.

On the next morning, Governor Young and his retinue appeared again. The Governor opened with a speech:

"Governor wants to be friend to all Indians whom he loves as a father and would give plenty clothes and good food provided they do not fight or slay white men."

Then he showed Wakara the presents he had brought. There were sixteen oxen, large quantities of cloth, blankets, dye and other things including powder for their guns. It was the Mormon belief that if the Indians got gunpowder they would not use it for killing white men unless provoked to do so. They felt that the Indians would more probably use it to obtain food.

All waited for the Chief's answer. It came to a silent, attentive audience.

"Wakara talk to Great Spirit. Great Spirit say, 'Make peace with white man.' Wakara say, 'White man Americats come and kill wife and children. Wakara no kill Gunnison. Governor say Wakara kill Gunnison. Wakara three hundred miles away.' Great Spirit say, 'Make peace.' "

Wakara added: "Wakara make peace. Listen to Great Spirit. If Indian kill white man again, Wakara make Indian howl like wolf."

The white men kept silent like their Indian counterparts but one could feel the relief in the minds of the white men present.

The peace pipe was passed round and the council

dissolved. Wakara gave the party an honor guard to the next village.

Solomon was well satisfied. He had been able to make several drawings including such chiefs as Ammon, Squash Head and Grosepine.

19 *The Hated Hornadoes*

It was eight hundred miles from Salt Lake City to San Bernardino and the entire trip was a journey through all kinds of climates and all kinds of terrains from the mild and pleasant to the hot and uncomfortable. Solomon, who was always philosophizing, said it was nature's way of teasing the traveler or perhaps nature's way of driving him hard and then letting down on the pressure. The route showed nature at its best and its worst.

It was the dreaded "hornado" that now awaited Solomon Carvalho with all its cruel tricks. A hornado was the worst punishment that man and beast could be subjected to. The word itself came from the Spanish word for "day" and men experienced in desert travel planned their journey so that it would be done in one stage consisting of one day. If anyone did stop in the desolate region, the animals would refuse to start again, so the traveler did not dare to halt on the way.

No man would have been able to bear the desert if it had consisted of one region instead of being broken up into many deserts with green valleys and rivers between them. The well-watered valley or little stream made a pause that gave the men the energy to continue. At each stop they would stock up on water, filling every canteen and dish and bottle to take with them. There was also the opportunity for everyone to enjoy a well-earned bath and wash away the dust and dirt of the journey.

If the shaded parts and valleys were comfortable, they had their own problems. Behind trees and rocks, Indians could and did lurk. The names of the Indian tribes changed as they journeyed through Utah and Nevada and finally California, but the danger remained.

At the beginning of the trip out of Salt Lake City, Solomon passed places he remembered from his trip with Fremont. At the Sevier River, he saw lumber lying in the lake which Fremont's party thought had been cut by men. At the time they believed that they had at last come to a village and that they were saved. The Delawares told them the bitter truth. The lumber had been cut by the beavers for their dams.

The Mormons in the party now used these logs to

make a raft to transport their wagons across the water. A bridge built by their engineers had been washed away in the spring floods.

They came to the Wasatch mountains where the party had been lost in the snows until Fremont took them back and gave them life again. However the Virgin and Santa Clara rivers which they followed soon after made them forget the tragic march. The valley was a riot of beautiful colors because of the multitude of wild flowers.

Then the flowers gave way to palm trees called "Spanish Needle," and the land became pebbly. The travelers knew that the character of the land would change again and hoped that the change would come soon. The pebbles which entered the hooves of the mule and donkey caused great discomfort to the animals. Moreover, the pebbles made the wagons jolt badly so that the people in them shook all over.

Again a pleasant valley, where this time Solomon bought a bow and arrows. The bow was made from one horn of a big horned sheep and the arrows were tipped with flint and obsidian. Solomon watched with a sick fascination as the Pahute Indians chewed the sinews of the deer to make a glue to put on the bow to make it stronger. He acquired a number of souvenirs from the Indians of the region which he knew would please David when he got home.

Solomon shopped for these primitive weapons, little knowing that there were other Indians on the bluffs high over the canyon ready to shoot him with their modern rifles.

For the Indians they met on the journey, Solomon had pity. They were naked and they dug for roots, which they ate together with lizards and snakes of the desert.

On the way they met again with high land and the fourteen horses were needed to pull each wagon over the high bluffs one at a time. On the tableland itself, they found again a flinty road and that was followed once more by grass and water.

Because the journey taxed their strength, the travelers from time to time would allow themselves a rest for a whole day. Their last hornado was to be a trip of fifty-five miles over an especially dry and hot desert, so they took a rest and began the trip at three o'clock in the morning. At midnight, they rested before continuing again in the early morning.

As they went along, they saw the usual signs of the hornado. Dead carcasses along the road showed the suffering of the animals. It became a horrible game to count the numbers of dead animals. They saw, too, furniture and feather beds which had been thrown out in attempt to lighten the load for the animals.

At the next stop on the Las Vegas River, they met a party of Mormons from San Bernardino who had halted their expedition to send some of their party back to the village for replacements for the horses and mules which had died on the way. They met, too, Peg-Leg Smith, the leader of a party of gold miners from the Colorado River. This old prospector told stories that were impossible to believe. He told them, among other things, that he had been in this part of the Californias in the year 1824. They found this hard to accept as true. However, he was an amusing and entertaining story teller who enlivened a dull and uncomfortable trip, so they listened to his stories and enjoyed them.

The hornadoes which followed became worse. The second one through the Mojave Desert was especially miserable. The hot wind blew up the lime soil, which entered their eyes, noses and lungs. The travelers coughed and choked. Solomon was fortunate in having a pair of goggles and he got a scarf to put over his nose and mouth.

Solomon's poor mule really suffered. It lost thirty pounds in forty-eight hours. They were glad to come to the next oasis—a lovely valley with wild grapes and colored birds of many kinds. This prepared them for the next stage—another hornado of thirty-one miles with only muddy water from a river bottom to quench their thirst.

When it seemed that the journey would never end, the travelers were pleased and relieved to arrive at the Tulare Pass which was the entrance to the San Bernardino Mountains. They found the pass quite pleasant, perhaps because they knew that their long journey was now practically over.

Once past the San Bernardino Mountains, they

found a pleasant agricultural land. The Mormons had built a fine village of comfortable cabins and had the usual cattle, fields of grain and saw and flour mills.

Solomon saw that his mule was completely exhausted and could go no further. He left it in the village and bought another for his travels to Los Angeles.

For twelve hours he followed a well-defined trail through mustard grass to the town of Los Angeles.

◼ After the Adventure

20 *All Israel is Responsible for One Another*

Joseph Newmark, Los Angeles merchant, turned in at the narrow stairs outside an adobe building at the corner of Commercial and Main streets. With him was Solomon Carvalho. A crudely lettered sign on unbleached muslin read "Moses Searles, Daguerreotypes," and a showcase to the right of the entrance showed some of the artist's pictures. Besides the usual studies of the ladies of the time, there were photos of the Californians who had been bitten by "the gold bug." There they stood for their relatives to admire—in mining dress, tattered and torn, each with his terrible revolver, the handle protruding menacingly from the holster. The curling moustaches and the beards told plainly that they had become miners in the true tradition of the Californias, and atop of it all was the Mexican sombrero.

Up the steps went the two. Inside the gallery they saw the usual headrest to keep the client in position, and a backdrop of plain bluish-gray material. Above the gallery was a skylight to catch the sun.

Newmark turned to his new-made friend. "This reminds you of home, I suppose."

Solomon Carvalho laughed. In his own gallery, the equipment was much more elaborate, but this was pioneer country and the competition was not quite so keen. So there was no need for fancy fixtures and ornaments.

The man who greeted them was dressed in the dark suit and white shirt of the typical Los Angeles businessman. He knew Mr. Newmark and had heard that there was a visitor in town. He was glad to learn that this visitor was of his own profession. Moses Searles had learned the trade while living in the city of Los Angeles and he was eager to meet this professional from whom he might learn something which would be helpful in his work.

Carvalho, on his part, had been told about Searles and he was amazed. "You are a very clever man, Mr. Searles, to be able to pick up this skill. I am told that you found out about the processing of copper plates though you had never had a lesson in chemistry and had never served in a photographer's gallery or processing room."

"I am afraid that I had to learn the hard way,"

answered Moses Searles. "It is Dr. Osburn who should get the credit. I had no schooling in chemistry. In fact, I had only three years in an elementary school when I went to work for my father as a painter. Dr. Osburn of this city put all the information before me and helped me when I found the struggle too much for my poor brain."

"You know, of course, that there are some rather good daguerreotypers living in San Francisco," said Solomon. "They have often displayed their work in, and written articles for, our magazine, the *Journal*."

"Yes," said Moses Searles. "I find the magazine very helpful and it serves to keep me informed of the new things that are being done by others in the field."

Mr. Newmark rose. "You may not be aware, Mr. Searles, that this is the man who came through the Rockies with. . . ."

Mr. Searles did not allow him to finish the sentence. "With Colonel Fremont! Imagine! I never dreamed that I would have the privilege of meeting a man so famous. Mr. Carvalho is a credit to our profession. The whole country will know about our state and when the pictures are published, we can hope for many, many more men like you in this territory, Mr. Carvalho."

Mr. Newmark smiled.

"There, you see, Mr. Carvalho. Every Californian becomes a one-man booster for the new state. Perhaps Mr. Searles will be able to do what I could not do. Perhaps he can persuade you to stay with us and help build this city."

Carvalho, half in jest said, "But if I come here, I would become a competitor to you in your business."

Mr. Newmark spoke out on his favorite topic.

"Mr. Carvalho, I predict that there will be work and to spare for two and even ten daguerreotypers. Los Angeles is destined to become, in not many more years, a world center, prominent in every field of human endeavor. I am quoting the words of my younger brother who, though he has just arrived from our native Prussia, is convinced from his knowledge of business in Europe that there is a great future in store for us."

"Of course," said Mr. Searles, "we will have to get rid of the mud on our streets and we will have to clean the roads in which people persist in throwing their rubbish and old shoes."

Mr. Newmark didn't like the implied criticism.

"This is a slight matter," he said. "We have already hired a zanjero who takes care of the water in the canals so that we can drink and cook with it without fear of illness. That is the first step our Council has taken for cleanliness. We will very shortly have someone to take care of the roads."

Mr. Carvalho said, "I find your city entirely delightful."

Then, turning to Mr. Searles, "I should like to see some of the work you have done. You have had the good fortune to photograph men who are laying the foundation of a great state on the Pacific Ocean."

Mr. Searles said, "I am proud to belong to the society of men who are helping to record history. I once read in the *Journal* of the daguerreotypists that the photo should preserve the remembrance of the past."

Mr. Carvalho said, "I agree. That was said by the editor himself, Mr. Humphreys. He is a very clever man."

Mr. Newmark excused himself.

"I must go back to my place of business," he said. "Solomon, do not lose your way in our big metropolis. I will be waiting for you at the store so we can go back to my casa for dinner together."

The two photographers were left together. Mr. Searles showed Solomon the photos he had taken of the prominent people in the young city; among them Solomon identified several as Jews. He saw the Newmarks, Jacob Elias and Solomon Lazard, as well as the talented Mrs. Jacob Rich, the first Jewish woman to settle in the city. Many of these founders of the city were known to him as business associates of the Newmarks, among them Colonel Banning and the Lanfranco brothers.

"Your pictures must go to every part of the world," said Solomon.

"Indeed they do," answered the photographer. "Mr. Jones here is from Australia and the Lanfranco brothers are from Genoa, Italy. Yes, these pictures will go all over the world to show relatives from far and near about this golden state."

Mr. Carvalho said good-bye to the gallery with its familiar smell of iodine that accompanied him out to the very street.

"These Californians," he said to himself. "Whatever topic you begin to talk about, they will soon find a way to tie it in with their state."

And as he crossed a rut in the main road, he thought, If I had talked about camels, he would have found a way to turn the conversation to the Golden Bear State.

Then he laughed as he remembered.

"Oh, no, they are bringing in some camels to see whether they can be used as desert transportation."

"I guess there must be something to a place if everyone is so enthusiastic about it," he said to himself as he opened the door to the dry goods store operated by the Newmarks.

21 *The Charter*

That evening the dinner party for the eastern visitor
was in the best tradition of Spanish hospitality. The
house itself was an adobe brick, one-story building
with many rooms opening on the patio. The doors
were wide and the windows deep and there were
shutters on them. Verandas all round the house
helped to keep the place cool and served to take
away from the drabness of the architecture.

Mrs. Newmark was English-born and had good
taste and an air of breeding which was also reflected
in her daughter Sarah's manner. Solomon was delighted with the young lady, especially since she bore
the same name as his wife.

They were served by a Chinese servant, who, Mrs.
Newmark pointed out, was the first of his people in
the pueblo. The dishes served were mostly of the

Mexican type but Mrs. Newmark had added some of the Jewish variety to please the guest of honor. The kugel, of her own making, was especially to Solomon's taste. For dessert, they had watermelon. Solomon expressed delight.

Mr. Newmark explained: "The watermelon or sandia as it is called, is one of the few fruits available as yet in this country—that and the cactus."

Mr. Newmark explained that though wild, the cactus pear was sweet and enjoyable.

"Well," said Solomon, "I ate the cactus, but in a different form from the way you serve it. When we were hungry on our journey, we were glad to find some cactus needles under the snow and to grind them for food."

At this, several of the men told of their own hardships while on their journey to California. Mr. Lazard related the time he crossed the jungle of Nicaragua and the younger Newmark told how he had bought a big bottle of whisky because he had been warned not to drink any of the water there. They all laughed as he told how he had to throw away the bottle as there was not enough room on his mule for both himself and the demijohn.

While they were at dinner, the bell rang out from the belfry of the old church of Our Lady of the Angels. Mr. Labatt explained that this was the eight o'clock curfew for Mexicans and Indians who might shoot up the town if they stayed out late drinking at the bars. Mr. Samuel Labatt came in as his brother was speaking. He had been unable to free himself earlier from his business and had come for the rest of the evening. The arrival of the younger Labatt and the tolling of the bell reminded everybody that this evening had been planned for a purpose.

For Mrs. Newmark this meeting of the men was an answer to a prayer. As a Jewish mother she had been vexed by a problem. The Jewish population was growing and yet there was no meeting place for the community and none of those things which Jews need to live as Jews.

"It is not only the living I worry about," she said. "Suppose someone should die. We do not have a burial place in case of need."

All were concerned about it, but nothing had been done. In 1850 a census showed that there had been six Jews in Los Angeles at that time, but they were transient and not even their names had been recorded. Now with the coming of families, there would be a stable community and they would have to establish an organization to serve their needs.

"This is exactly what we have already told Mr. Carvalho," said her husband, "and he has encouraged us to begin organizing."

"There is not a great deal to the organization of a community," said Solomon. "All one needs is the desire. If you wish, I can help draw up a constitution for such a group. It could, if you wish, resemble that of the city of Baltimore."

That night was the beginning of the organization

called the Hebrew Benevolent Society, the first social agency of Los Angeles. Solomon Carvalho left
no doubt in the minds of the Jewish community
that he had the necessary experience. Every detail
was seen to.

The constitution stated in detail the officers to be
chosen, the duties of each, the fees to be paid by
members and the time of meeting. The prime objec-
tive of this group, of course, was to help one another
in time of need. Solomon made it easy for those in
need to acquire the money and help necessary. No
one who was ill or in trouble was to have to wait or
appear before a large committee and thus be shamed
publicly. A letter or a visit to the chairman of the
Charity Committee would be sufficient to bring results. In the case of illness, the chairman was himself
to go immediately to give aid either in money or in
other forms of assistance.

Within a week the Burial Committee had bought
a plot for a cemetery, to be called the "Home of
Peace," in the quiet environment of Lilac Terrace
and Lookout Drive. The name and the place seemed
to be in perfect harmony. Even Nathan Tuch, who
was married to a full-blooded Indian squaw and was
not especially interested in the Jewish religion, became a member of the society. He was later buried
in the plot by his loving and respected wife. Thirty
charter members signed their names to the constitution
document.

Next day the *Los Angeles Star* (*La Estrella de Los*

Angeles) carried a notice of the formation of the society. Since news was scarce, the paper was glad to devote considerable space to the event. The editors, John A. Lewis and John McElroy hoped for the day when the telegraph would come through. Their dependence on stage and steamer for their news could be embarrassing. They remembered with a shudder that the news of the deaths of Webster and Clay had taken a full month to arrive. Yes, the news of the society got good coverage in the sleepy little town paper.

Altogether, Carvalho felt that he had had an interesting and profitable day. He had resumed contact with his two chief interests at home. First, he had rubbed shoulders with someone in his own line of business, and secondly, he had spent an evening improving the situation of a growing Jewish community. This sort of thing came with civilization—where men joined together for mutual aid. In the mountains, although leadership was important, a man had to make it alone on his own ability to withstand the elements. Community progress came when men of good will learned to stand and work together.

22 *Mr. Solomon Nunes Carvalho, Author*

It was August, 1856, and Solomon Carvalho was again a business visitor in the home of Colonel Fremont, this time by arrangement with Mrs. Jessie Benton Fremont.

Mrs. Fremont, her usual gracious self, asked Solomon about the health of his wife and family and whether Solomon was settled once again in his profession as a photographer.

Solomon assured her that the family was well and that though he was back in his studio in Baltimore, he was bored and found his work hopelessly dull. He gave the impression that the trip had spoiled him for his previous routine and that he would welcome something a little more interesting in the future.

Solomon then congratulated Mrs. Fremont on the Colonel's nomination to the presidency. He said that in his mind he was certain that she would be the next First Lady in the White House.

Mrs. Fremont laughed.

"There will have to be a lot of hard work first and we are hoping that all the Colonel's friends will find the time and the desire to make the campaign a successful one."

Solomon agreed and said: "Mrs. Fremont, it is my feeling that a book telling about the fifth expedition would be helpful in bringing the party success. I do think that the public should be told about the leadership qualities of the man who is heading the Republican party. Those of us who were fortunate to be with the Colonel learned to recognize his ability to overcome every difficulty. It is my belief that the American people should be told about this."

Mrs. Fremont listened attentively.

"I should like to read you some of the impressions that I wrote to my wife and which I would include in the book."

Mrs. Fremont nodded her head for him to go on.

"Personal courage and skill he showed at all times and fairness to those who worked with him. Through every difficulty and in every situation, he showed self-control. He stood out bravely against all difficulties. We, on our part, feeling his strength, became stronger and were able to stand the sufferings of the trip. The Colonel's worst enemies must agree that he had the ability to inspire his men to great deeds. We, who continued with him on this journey despite all difficulties, are the actual proof of this," Solomon read from his letters.

"That is beautiful, Mr. Carvalho," said Mrs. Fremont.

In the next hour Solomon Carvalho discussed with Mrs. Fremont several details about the book. It was arranged that Mr. Bigelow be approached to publish it, since he was already the publisher of a biography about the Colonel. Mrs. Fremont offered her New York home as a place where Solomon could develop the prints, and suggested that, since he would be very busy, he ask Mathew Brady and another Philadelphia artist, Philip Hamilton, to help.

There was still one more request that Solomon had to make.

"This book is intended to be a tribute to a noble character and to show how one man can inspire others to great deeds. I should therefore like to honor his wife, also. I would be pleased if you would allow me to dedicate this book to you."

This was a gallant gesture and Mrs. Fremont thanked him gracefully.

Before leaving, Solomon told Mrs. Fremont that he had actually been the first to think about the Colonel as the future president of the United States. He told about the camp on the Kansas River, when the men were waiting for the Colonel to come and begin the march. It had been a successful day of buffalo hunting and the men were greatly impressed by the richness of this land. They had had a feast of small, sweet wild grapes, which they got by pulling the vine from the bottom, Indian fashion.

Afterward, sitting round the campfire, stomachs full, they had begun talking about the immensity of the country and the man best suited to open it to settlement. Naturally, it would have to be a man who knew the land well, who had convictions that it should be opened up and who had the leadership necessary to see that this was done. But most of all the men said that this leader would have to believe in a slave-free nation.

At that campfire, Solomon Carvalho nominated John Charles Fremont for the position and the men, with a mighty shout, voted for him unanimously.

Jessie Fremont liked the story.

"It seems that you were also a prophet," she said.

Solomon left the house in good spirits. He found himself humming a popular campaign song which was sweeping the country:

> Rise up, Fremont, and go before,
> The hour must have its man,
> Put on the hunting shirt once more
> And lead Freedom's van.

A young woman passed him on the street. She was dressed in a violet muslin dress of the type which Jessie favored and her hair was combed back simply over her ears like Mrs. Fremont's.

She smiled at Solomon and responded with another verse:

> She shall be our Liberty's queen
> And he shall rule over the state
> From mountains of granite and green
> To the land of the Golden Gate.

There was optimism everywhere. Fremont would be the president—some little reward for all he had done for his country.

23 *Free Soil, Free Speech, and Fremont*

"What a busybody! What a blasted busybody!"

Jacob Ritterband, nephew of Sarah Carvalho, was coming out of a shop on Third Street in Philadelphia when he expressed himself in these words. He was on his rounds, calling on customers. He had heard someone speaking out in a loud voice and that voice sounded familiar. When he looked to where the voice came from, he saw a familiar figure standing on the curb. Sure enough, it was Solomon Carvalho.

"Well, at least he has taken that ever-present cigar out of his mouth," thought Jacob.

Jacob resented his uncle. He resented his careful dress, his impeccable grooming, and the way he was always aware of himself. In fact, he hated everything about this uncle-by-marriage. He knew without ask-ing that his uncle's bags would be at this moment standing in the spare bedroom. He must have come up on the train to spend a day or so with the family while on business in Philadelphia. These days the "business" lay not so much in the photographic trade as in his new political interests.

Jacob's eyes took in the type of people surround-ing the speaker.

"Idlers!" he thought to himself. "Like Carvalho. Always worrying about the world."

He was familiar with their habits of heckling and arguing with any man who would dare to stand up on the street corner to address a crowd. Jacob stepped behind the shadow of a large elm tree to listen, hop-ing that his uncle would be "cut down to size" by some smart aleck.

His uncle was in the middle of a long speech.

"Ladies and Gentlemen," he said, "it is our duty to put this man in the White House. Each and every one of you must go to the polls to make sure that the Republican ticket wins. This new party will find leadership and direction in the hands of this leader of men."

It didn't take long for the hecklers to find some-thing to heckle about.

"That's not the way they tell it round here," spoke up one of the idlers who had ambled over to listen and enjoy the fun. "How about the court-martial? You don't expect much from a man who can't take orders. Fremont refused to take orders from his commanding officer. A man that can't take orders, can't give orders, say I."

Solomon took the question seriously. It was one of the criticisms which Fremont met everywhere.

"What would you do if two superior officers were giving you orders at the same time?" said Solomon. "General Kearney and General Stockton were each pulling his own way and Colonel Fremont was in the middle of it all. What would you have done? Whom would you have obeyed?"

Solomon returned to the theme of his speech.

"Here is a man accustomed to leadership. In this man we find dignity and honesty."

Again an interruption from someone in the crowd.

"What's the story about his mother? That's not very dignified."

"Shame," said Solomon. "Are you going round to spread that gossip? Why let scandal lose us a fine man? I don't care about his family. No honest American cares about family. We left all that behind us in Europe. Here in America a man is what he makes himself. No nobility or poppycock of that kind. We are a republic and we believe in the equality of man. Colonel Fremont's mother left an old man, a husband who would not give her a divorce, to start a new life with a young French immigrant of good character and intelligence. Are you going to blame Fremont for that?"

"Well, do you deny that he is Catholic and was

married by a Catholic priest?" Another voice was joining in the fun.

"Catholic?" Solomon said with no surprise in his voice. "Don't listen to these rumors. That is what the Democratic party wants you to believe. It is spreading these rumors because it is afraid that this man, by the force of his personality, will carry the nation. He's gaining strength in all parts of the country and the Democrats are on the run."

Solomon warmed up to his subject.

"Let's look at the work of this man—accomplished at a very young age. He is the man who took California for the United States of America. He is the man who warned us that England and Russia stood ready to grab the Golden State when and if Mexico would leave it. And he was the man who was ready and on the spot to see that California would be American.

"And having done this, he was the man who made it possible for the emigrant wagons to find their way to that golden land. With the information and maps he drew, the way to the West was clear for all. Is it any wonder that President Polk remitted the penalty of the court-martial and ordered Colonel Fremont back to his duties in the American Army?"

"Ladies and gentlemen," Solomon said, warming up. "Colonel Fremont faced great danger both as an explorer and politically. Never has any man faced greater odds. Yet in spite of all, he has succeeded. Having opened the way to California, he became its first senator. And during his short term of office, he was able to pass many laws which were helpful to the new state. He took care of the Indians, he took care that land titles would be safe, he even made sure that there would be a university very soon."

"But even his old man won't vote for him," came another catcall.

"Yes, that is sad but true," said Solomon. "But what would you expect from old Rhinoceros-Hide Benton? The Senator is a dyed-in-the-wool Democrat and nothing will move him from his party. If he could see how the Republican party will save America from slavery, he'd not be Democrat very long. As for me," Solomon added, "I am for free soil, free speech and Fremont."

He ended his speech and Jacob realized that he had better go before Solomon had a chance to see him. Jacob went off to serve his customers. He dreaded the next few days when Uncle Solomon would be a guest at his house. His wife would insist on that. She and the children would listen to him tell of his adventures with Fremont.

"As for myself," mumbled Jacob as he hurried on, "I will agree with General Grant who said, 'I don't know what kind of president Buchanan will make, but I know Fremont and therefore will vote for Buchanan.' If Uncle Solomon is for Fremont, I'm for Buchanan."

He sniffed as he went along.

"The two of them, Fremont and his photographer

—large bubbles of vanity. What a pity they weren't both lost in the Rockies—or at least that they didn't stay on the other side of the Rockies. This country is big enough for that.

"I suppose that Carvalho is expecting a good fat political job out of it if Fremont wins."

Solomon was left with a few of the bystanders who by now had recognized him as the photographer who had been with Fremont on his last trip in 1853.

One of the youths was especially interested. He was a butcher's assistant who had saved up enough money to go to California. He hoped that there would be a chance for him to do well there.

"Is it true that the Colonel is sending out hundreds of pounds of gold in buckskin bags from his mine in the Mariposa?" he asked.

Solomon assured him that this was true.

"Could I find gold like that?" was what the young man wanted to know next.

Again Solomon assured him that everything was possible in that wonderful land.

There was still another question in the mind of the boy.

"Would I find any trouble because I am Jewish?"

Solomon was glad to let the boy know that he need have no fears on that count.

"The Colonel chose me even though he could tell from my name that I am a Sephardi Jew. I had no trouble finding friends among the expeditionary party nor even among the Indians. It is time that we Jews learn that all men, whether Jew or Gentile, are equal. We must move with the times. We must take our place as Americans. We have a responsibility in shaping the future of our glorious country."

Solomon left the young man with addresses of several people in the city of Los Angeles, and once more assured him that everything would go well for him. He told him about the synagogue there and asked him to carry a personal regard to Rabbi Eckman, the spiritual guide of the synagogue.

Solomon was proud that he had had some share in organizing the Jewish community of Los Angeles.

He went on his way and suddenly remembered that he had not asked the young man which route he was taking to the West.

"Oh, well," thought Solomon, "I suppose he won't take the emigrant trail. He'll probably go there by way of the Panama Railroad. Not everyone is ready to face the hardships of the trail.

"Anyway, I hope that he does vote for the Colonel."

And as an afterthought, Solomon added, "That is, if he is old enough to vote."

24 *Looking Backward*

Professor and Mrs. Carvalho were enjoying a holiday in Bermuda. To Solomon this was one of the places he had always wanted to revisit. As a young man, before he was out of his teens, he had come here to live with his uncle David, who owned a shipping company. It was here that he had been considered a bit of a hero, when he swam out with a rope tied round his waist to help a boat that was stranded on the rocks. Then, while the passengers were sent ashore from his uncle's boat, he sat in a breeches buoy and amused himself by drawing pictures of some of the interesting scenes in the rescue.

Life had never been dull for Solomon. Things did not always turn out as expected. Had Fremont been elected, Solomon felt that his reward would have been some good political job for his efforts. After all, some of his letters to Sarah had been included in the campaign booklet which had been written by John Bigelow and had helped to boost the Colonel's cause.

But a man has to be ready for reverses. And when the Colonel lost the election to Buchanan, Solomon had turned to a growing field in American engineering called thermodynamics. Engineering had found a new way to heat American houses and offices. One need no longer depend on fireplaces or Benjamin Franklin stoves. The Carvalho Heating and Super-Heating firm of New York City would send in a crew of men with pipes and radiators that could remodel the whole house and make it modern.

In starting such a business Solomon had shown again that man with a fertile brain can always make a living. And when his patents were accepted by the Patent Office in Washington. Carvalho gave himself the title of "Professor Carvalho."

In this new line of business, Solomon had done well and he was proud to think that he had been able to give his sons good educations. Little David, who had watched his father pack before the trip, had entered the field of chemistry and was also considered a world-famous handwriting expert. He achieved international fame when he demonstrated clearly that the documents in the Dreyfus case in France were forgeries and not the work of Captain Dreyfus. Solomon was proud that his son had served the cause of justice well in rebutting this slander against an innocent Jew.

Solomon, for his part, had never stopped working for his community. He had the honor of presiding at a banquet in 1858 at which the Jews of Baltimore honored British Jewry on the occasion of the entry of a Jew into the British Parliament. Solomon, as an American, was proud of the fact that American Jewry had preceded the British in gaining this privilege of being elected as representatives of the people to Congress.

Through the years Solomon followed the career of his beloved Colonel with interest. He was proud that the Colonel while in Europe had been able to buy arms for the Union Army, though this was not generally known by many people. He was proud that Fremont had been a well-known public figure when Abraham Lincoln was still a little-known lawyer from a small town in Illinois. He was proud that the Colonel had the foresight to predict the Civil War and had warned the public a year before the outbreak of the Civil War. He was proud that the Colonel, now General, had made a proclamation freeing the slaves in the army under his command long before the Emancipation Proclamation of Lincoln was issued. And finally he was proud that the Colonel had seen the railroad built through the Rockies.

Whenever the words "the colonel" were used, there could be no doubt which colonel was meant. Like Richard H. Dana, who wrote *Two Years Before the Mast*, Solomon believed that "there are many colonels in America, but when anyone says, 'the colonel,' there is no doubt that they mean Colonel Fremont."

There was one other place that Solomon would have liked to see again—California, which had a special place in his heart. He would have liked to take the Santa Fe Railroad there, but his family demanded all his time. However, he often received letters from Rabbi Julius Eckman who had been the first rabbi in California.

About his book Solomon could afford to laugh now, though at the time it had been painful to him. The publishers, Derby and Jackson, had offered him three hundred dollars or five cents for every copy sold. Solomon, who was in need of money at the time, and thinking that this would be the better proposition, chose the first sum. Imagine his surprise when the book went through four printings plus a British edition. Had he chosen the latter proposition, he would have made five times the amount.

However, money isn't everything. What disappointed Solomon more than anything else was that his daguerreotypes—the hundreds for which he had suffered—had not been widely published. They had been dug from the snows in Utah and brought to Washington, but nothing had come of them. A few of them had been put into his book, some of them had been destroyed by fire, but for the most part they lay buried under a pile of material in the National

Archives in Washington, D.C. Solomon felt that a part of him had been destroyed. Much of his work and suffering had been wasted.

There were, of course, other compensations. In his community he had been appreciated. Many honors had been given him in recognition of his work. The Maryland Historical Society had chosen him for membership in their organization. To them he lectured often, telling them of the grand and glorious adventure which he had shared with a brave company headed by a heroic figure—the Colonel.

The Talmud speaks out very clearly to every man with the clear direction: "Do not separate yourself from your community."

Solomon was satisfied that he had done his share both as a Jew and as an American. He had never separated himself from his community.